# Digital Character Design and Painting:

## The Photoshop® CS Edition

# Digital Character
# Design and Painting:
## The Photoshop® CS Edition

**DON SEEGMILLER**

**CHARLES RIVER MEDIA, INC.**

**Hingham, Massachusetts**

Publisher: Jenifer Niles
Cover Design: The Printed Image
Cover Images: Don Seegmiller

CHARLES RIVER MEDIA, INC.
10 Downer Avenue
Hingham, Massachusetts 02043
781-740-0400
781-740-8816 (FAX)
info@charlesriver.com
www.charlesriver.com

This book is printed on acid-free paper.

Don Seegmiller. *Digital Character Design and Painting: The Photoshop CS Edition.*
ISBN: 1-58450-340-8

Library of Congress Cataloging-in-Publication Data
Seegmiller, Don.
   Digital character design and painting : the Photoshop CS edition / Don Seegmiller.—
Photoshop CS ed., 1st ed.
      p.  cm.
   ISBN 1-58450-340-8 (pbk. : alk. paper)
1. Computer graphics.    2. Adobe Photoshop.    I. Title.
   T385.S366 2004
   776--dc22

Printed in the United States of America
06  7  6  5  4  3

This book is dedicated to my family; in particular, my children
who have always helped keep my vision clear
and my perspective correct.

# CONTENTS

# PREFACE

Why strive to be an artist? There are certainly easier ways to make a living, and there are definitely better-paying vocations. Combine those two points with the fact that most artists are not at all satisfied with the end results of their efforts and the question almost becomes absurd. Why on earth would anyone want to do this? Why does someone continue with an activity or profession when a sense of failure or disappointment with the final product is so common? If you were an air traffic controller or surgeon and failed to reach your goal at the end of each landing or surgery, I doubt you could continue in that profession. Why, then, do we keep trying to do this? I really think that there is only one reason that we persevere in our efforts: we love the feeling that the process of creating art instills within us. It is the travel and not the destination that we love. Professional artists or not, we feel the same inner reward when we are in the process of creating art, and this alone is reason enough to continue to struggle and call ourselves artists.

I myself am an artist through and through. I just cannot seem to control myself. Give me a crayon at a restaurant and I will draw on the tablecloth. I carry a sketch book with me always. My hands permanently smell like turpentine. For as long as I can remember, this need to draw and paint has been part of my existence. As for a label, you may call me a professional artist in as much as creating art is how I support my family and lifestyle. Up until 1995, I was only a "traditional" artist. I painted in oil and sold the paintings through a very traditional art gallery. Never had I seriously considered the possibility of doing art on a computer, and yet I remember vividly in the late '70s going into an art supply store and seeing a massive machine in the corner. It was a computer, and the darn thing could make pictures. As I look back, the pictures were not very sophisticated, being mostly primitive shapes filled with colors or gradients, and the output was on Polaroid™ film. Nevertheless, it did not matter that the machine was as big as a small car or that it cost as much as a small house. I was hooked on digital art. The possibilities seemed endless.

Here it is a new millennium. Computers are small enough to be easily carried when you are traveling, imaging programs have now reached a level where virtually anything is possible, and movies, games, the Internet, television, and even the printed media are relying more and more on digital imagery to communicate ideas. It is now economically possible for artists of all experience levels to create digital content, and as an audience we are becoming more sophisticated in our demands on the quality of images we see. The future of art is here whether you like it or not.

So what does all this philosophy have to do with a book on character design and digital art? Plenty, I hope. What you have in your hand is my attempt to merge two distinct yet intimately interrelated subjects: character design and digital painting.

Character design is all about ideas and how to put those ideas together. Any time that you need to design a character, your mind starts spinning and the cogs start turning. You come up with ideas that will fulfill the client's vision but that are also merged with your thoughts and ideas. Possibly you are lucky and you only have to come up with ideas for yourself. Your ideas may be very concrete or amorphous. It really does not matter who you are designing for; the design process is all about ideas.

On the other hand, the digital painting process is about the combination of method, techniques, and artistic theory. It is all about how to do a "thing" and that thing is how to make something that is ultimately viewed in two dimensions imitate three dimensions. The subject is not only about the theory of how to make images in two dimensions but often how to create a specific effect in a specific application.

This book is about merging these two distinct subjects. Though different, neither of these subjects—character design and digital painting—can stand on its own. A great design is nothing if you can't communicate that idea to the audience; conversely, the most beautifully rendered image is nothing without a good idea.

This is the crux and solution to the problem at hand. Why not have a book that deals with both subjects? The first section could explain how to come up with great ideas, and the second could explain how to visualize those ideas so that others could appreciate their beauty. So here is that attempt at merging two very creative and different disciplines that nevertheless require each other to be successful.

The book is in three parts. Part I deals with character design and coming up with the ideas that are worth visualizing. Part II is a brief review of some traditional artistic principles that will improve your art skills when you incorporate them into digital painting. Part III shows you how to solve some of the visual problems that will always be present when you are painting digital art and specifically figurative character art.

There is only one reason for this book and that is to help you merge the differing disciplines of character design, the ever-expanding digital universe, and good old-fashioned artistic skill and creativity. This book has been written so that anyone from the seasoned professional to the aspiring artist will find something of use. Professionals will possibly find ideas for ways of doing things that had never occurred to them before. Aspiring artists will find valuable information on very basic artistic principles and specific techniques for designing a character. If you are neither a professional nor an aspiring artist, we hope that there is some art you will find intriguing to look at.

I found it rather difficult to write a book about the technique of digital art and how it merges with traditional principles because there is no definitive right or wrong way to create art. Almost everything that you find here is a result of my study and experience as a professional artist since the early '80s. The artistic ideas presented for the most part are not new but rather are as old as art itself. I have found that while we have been taught the same basic principles, sometimes the implementation of that knowledge is less well taught.

This book is similar and yet very different from the previous edition. While the first two sections of the book dealing with strategies, techniques, and fundamental artistic principles as applied to digital art have changed very little, the third part is completely new in both subject matter and technique.

1. Part I looks at strategies to help you come up with your initial ideas.
2. Part II discusses some fundamental artistic principles that are often overlooked in this digital world and how to incorporate them into your efforts.
3. Part III looks at some basic tutorials on painting on the computer. These are followed by in-depth tutorials on how to create more sophisticated paintings.

When all is said and done, I hope you will feel inspired by what you see and that this book will help you as you struggle to create and realize your own visions.

# About the Author

Don Seegmiller has been an artist as long as he can remember. Some of his earliest memories are of getting into trouble in school because he was drawing pictures in the margins on the math pages instead of doing the addition and subtraction.

In 1973, he was accepted into the Art Department at Brigham Young University on a talent scholarship. As with most artists, academics were of secondary importance to the drawn image, yet in the spring of 1979 he did graduate with a Bachelor of Fine Arts degree in Graphic Design, with a specialization in Illustration. He was promptly employed by one of the departments at the school as a graphic designer/illustrator. While employed at Brigham Young University, he decided that commercial deadlines were not what he wanted to be dealing with, so he became a fine artist. He began to paint egg tempera paintings in the evenings, and after trying various subject matter decided that his heart and talent were most at home with the human figure. In the fall of 1980, with three paintings under his arm, he traveled to Santa Fe, New Mexico, seeking representation in one of the many art galleries in town. His work has been shown in Wadle Galleries of Santa Fe since 1981. He has painted more than 500 oil paintings of the figure and is represented in public and private collections worldwide.

In the spring of 1995, two opportunities that could not be ignored presented themselves. He was asked to teach figure drawing at Brigham Young University for both the Fine Art Department and the Graphics Department. Since that time, the departments have merged and he continues to teach senior-level illustration, traditional head painting, figure drawing, and digital painting for the Department of Visual Design. He also joined the staff of Saffire Corporation, where he was the art director for six years. Saffire is a small developer of video games for publishers such as Nintendo, Electronic Arts, Titus, and Mindscape.

He is a regular speaker at the Game Developers Conference. In the spring of 2002, 2003, and 2004 he did full-day tutorials on character design and digital painting and creativity.

He was the keynote speaker at the American Association of Medical Illustrators convention in New Orleans in the summer of 2003. He has taught workshops at individual game developers around the country. He also has taught at the University of California, Irvine extension, and the Ringling School of Art in Sarasota, Florida.

He traveled for a while demonstrating Metacreations Painter 6 at the major trade shows. His work is featured in the *The Painter 6 Wow! Book, The Painter 7 Wow! Book, Electronic Step by Step Design, Spectrum 7, and Spectrum 8.*

He has written software reviews for the Web site *www.critical-depth.com* and for *Design Graphics* magazine.

He continues to pursue his traditional fine art, digital art, character design, and teaching passions.

# INTRODUCTION

Have you ever doodled creatures on the edges of the phone book while waiting for directory assistance? How many of you have scribbled on a scrap of paper while sitting in a boring meeting?

I would venture to say that almost everyone has at one time or another spent some time drawing the characters and monsters that populate our minds. For a few of us, this random doodling begins to become something more. We take these random images and expand on them until they are more fully realized. For even a smaller number, this drawing becomes a painting. For some, this compulsion to draw and paint the population of our mind ultimately becomes if not our vocation then an activity that we feel almost an obsession to engage in.

This book is for all people who have ever felt the need to put the images in their heads down into a more solid statement to share with others. There is something in this book for you whether you are a complete novice wondering where to begin to draw the characters of your imagination, or whether you are a seasoned professional looking for information to help improve your current skills.

The book is divided into three basic parts. Part I deals with ideas and is about things of a more cerebral nature. It covers such topics as how to get ideas and how to get them out so that others may see them. It serves as an outline for a method of turning on the tap in your brain and letting the ideas flow and develop. Artists of all levels should understand the chapters in this part.

Part II is about artistic fundamentals that will help you take your ideas to the next step: drawing and painting them so that others may appreciate your efforts. This part is laid out somewhat like a textbook and specifically focuses on things that seem difficult for both beginning and more advanced artists in their struggles with drawing and painting. In most areas, a basic understanding of artistic principles is not needed. Most subjects are covered so that both the beginning and more advanced artist will understand the concepts.

Part III is a series of demonstrations that show how I have handled different subject matter when drawing and painting. This part, which provides demonstrations and tutorials, does not give you an exact formula for duplicating what you are seeing but allows you to work along through the creation process and then use what you have learned in your own work.

## SOFTWARE AND HARDWARE REQUIREMENTS

This is a book on digital painting, so you need certain equipment in order to follow the demonstrations and exercises. You obviously need a computer with lots of hard drive space as well as a monitor capable of displaying at least 16-bit color. You will have greater success if you use some sort of stylus to use when painting. Painting with a mouse is possible but feels a lot like painting with a bar of soap.

As far as software, the author is using Photoshop CS. It's assumed that you have a fundamental understanding of this software. If you do not have Photoshop CS, Photoshop 7 will suffice. Earlier versions of Photoshop are not recommended as the brush engine in both CS and version 7 were significantly improved over earlier versions. In Part III, where the exercises appear, great detail on how to achieve a particular effect is not necessarily provided since this is not a Photoshop "how-to" section. Rather, Part III is more about getting into my brain and watching the process as each painting is completed.

Many other 2D applications will suffice if you do not own Photoshop CS. Be aware that you will not be able to reproduce the effects exactly, but you will be able to use the general principles discussed.

It is the author's hope that this book will serve you as you strive to be a better character designer and artist.

# CHARACTER DESIGN

A section of a book that is dedicated to character design is an unusual thing. Many books have had individual chapters that mention some aspect of character design, and some even go as far as having a few images supporting the text. This book is different. Part I of this book will give the reader a list of questions that every character designer must consider as they begin to create. Without considering all of these ideas, a character may be very creative, but if it does not fit the needs of the project then time has been wasted. Not only does this part pose the questions you must ask yourself as a character designer, but these chapters will give you some clear, concise, and creative methods for coming up with and improving your designs. Once you have the ideas, we'll explore how to improve on them and give your character a life of its own. Combine all these things and you, the reader, will have an arsenal of information and exercises never before presented in one volume.

As you go through Part I, try to use and remember some of this information as you create. Your character designs will be better for it.

# 1

# INTRODUCTION TO CHARACTER DESIGN

For as long as people have been telling stories (and, eventually, writing books), they have verbally and with the written word created different characters to populate their fictional worlds. The beauty and strength of many of these character descriptions is that much was left up to the listener's or reader's imagination. With the advent of television, movies, and now video games, however, things have changed. The medium is visually describing the characters and environments for us as an audience. While our perceptions will still be unique to each of us, those perceptions are now closer together than they have ever been.

As an audience, we are getting more sophisticated in our expectations of visual imagery. When we were children, Frankenstein (Figure 1.1) was quite terrifying. We had probably never seen such a frightening

**FIGURE 1.1**    The Frankenstein monster.

creature, and none of our childhood experiences could have caused us to imagine anything like it. The movie was trying to take over our imagination and make us see exactly what it wanted us to see.

Eventually, as we grew up, those creatures were no longer as frightening, and we wanted more scare for our movie dollar. In the early 1980s, *Star Wars* was released. Here was a whole universe based on one man's vision, and he wanted us to see exactly what he wanted us to see. To a large degree he succeeded, because we all know what Darth Vader looks like and we all equate him with evil. The desire of creators to have us see their individual vision carries on to this day in movies like *Tomb Raider*, where there is very little room for the leading actress to add to the character's personality. We already know what Laura Croft looks and acts like. Some of these characters are so strong that they actually become cultural icons. The original Frankenstein is a good example of a character's staying power.

Nowadays, there is less room for our imagination to create unique images within our heads when we are presented with such visually stunning creations. Increasingly characters are so well designed that the images and ideas they convey are relatively the same regardless of each viewer's background.

With this power to take over another's imagination for a short time comes a responsibility to do it well. You do not want to be remembered as the character designer of one of the silliest characters to ever grace the screen or monitor; you'd like to be renowned for creating one of the most memorable ones. Think back on some of the movies with characters that enthralled and disappointed you when you were younger. They could have scared you nearly to death, sent your imagination soaring, or seemed so ridiculous that you were either disappointed or bored. We all have our favorites. Some characters that had excellent character designs were those in the movies *Dark Crystal*, *Labyrinth*, and *Alien*, among many others.

On the other hand, there is a movie called *Robot Monster*, made way back in 1953. The main creature in the movie was a man in a gorilla suit who was wearing what looked like a cardboard, old-fashioned diving helmet, with car antennas glued to the side. It looked something like Figure 1.2.

It is so ridiculous that you can't help but laugh. This is definitely an example of bad character design.

Very little has been written on what direction you should take when designing characters for the screen, games, and print. This may very well be because we are so individual that it is hard to quantify what makes a good character. What is good character design for one individual may not be for another. Most of the character design process itself is based on rather ambiguous ideas of what is creative and what is not.

Have no doubt; character design is an art. The fleshing-out of a character is successful to a large degree when you apply traditional artistic principles to a creative idea. Most of us who desire to work in the entertainment industry

**FIGURE 1.2**    The "Robot Monster" sketch.

(whether in film, games, or something else) are just expected to know how to flesh out a character when we graduate from school. In addition, most of us just assume that because we can draw a dragon or an elf, we are character designers. After all, we have been drawing monsters, villains, soldiers, and heroes for as long as we can remember. The sad fact is, however, that artists, even good ones, are not necessarily good character designers.

Like all of the arts, character design has its own set of fundamental skills that if mastered will make artists better designers. Until very recently, most art schools did not offer a curriculum that dealt with the basics associated with good character design. This area is often overlooked in schools possibly because, as with many of the arts, there is no one way of doing something correctly in character design (as there is, say, in chemistry). The problem with this approach is that artists are left to their own devices to figure out their own working methods. This approach may work for some, but most of the time, artists spend a lot of wasted time and effort exploring dead-end avenues, and for many, there is no success without direction.

Most students want a set of rules or techniques that they can work on mastering. After mastering the basic skills, they then have more freedom to accept the premises taught, or they can reject them and explore their own directions. Almost always, success is quicker when you know and can work with some fundamental ideas.

For this reason, this section presents a series of "basic rules" that, if used, will improve your abilities as a character designer. Most of the ideas are not original in and of themselves. The uniqueness of this section lies in the fact that the ideas have rarely been combined together into one section on character design.

## WHAT IS CHARACTER DESIGN?

What is good character design? For that matter, what is character design? The art of character design is no more and no less than creating someone or something that, taken in the context of its environment, will elicit a belief, reaction, or expectation from the audience about the physical makeup, disposition, and personality of the creation. Why, then, is there such a wide diversity of good and bad character design when the premise is so simple? Figure 1.3 shows a blob, backlit, standing in a doorway.

Figure 1.4 represents something. Is it a well-designed character?

Figure 1.3 is not a character design. You have no expectations for the object and it does not elicit much emotional response. Figure 1.4, though

**FIGURE 1.3**    Is this a character design?

**FIGURE 1.4**    Is this more of a character design?

simple and only showing a shadow figure, nevertheless demands something from the viewer. You have expectations, whether right or wrong, about the character.

In today's high-tech environment, there should be no excuse for a bad character design as in the 1953 *Robot Monster* film. For the most part, we have the means and the budget to create good designs. Now it is up to us, the artists, to learn how to deliver a good design.

Along with the end goal of having a good design, we will always need to consider the practical issues of the character's design. The most visually appealing design in the world is worthless if it is not useful.

## Character Design Issues and Limitations

So let's talk about some of the practical issues and limitations that are associated with a character's design. You must be aware of many issues as you work on a character design. Often, you will be able to sit down with the animators and modelers and get precise specifications for their needs. Other times, you will not have this contact and will need to know what general questions to ask so that the character will be correctly designed for its specific use or platform. Over time and with experience, you will gain general knowledge of what is expected and what the parameters are for a given platform. Not too long ago, a character of 1,000 polygons was very detailed for one of the current game platforms. If you didn't know this information (or didn't ask some of the correct questions about the limits of the platform you were working for), you, the modelers, and animators could either be in for a long and stressful project or it would be a very short relationship.

The following sections cover some issues and limitations that you as a character designer must be aware of before you start and as you work. The questions are only posed; solutions are not given on purpose because the questions and solutions will probably be different for each assignment.

### How Will the Character Be Used?

You need to know if the character will appear as a supporting background object, a mid-ground prop, a foreground character, or the center of interest. A character that is closer to the camera generally needs more finesse and detail, but maybe not the same level of detail as a character at the same distance but that is the center of focus. The human vision is very selective, and things on the periphery of our awareness will not need to be complicated.

### How Will the Character Be Displayed?

Quite obviously, the needs associated with the different media vary widely. A character in print will require much more detail than a character on the movie screen. A character for a movie will need more detail than a character on a video or television monitor. A TV or video character will need much more detail than a character on a handheld game.

### How Close or Distant to the Camera Will the Character Be?

If the character will never be closer to the viewer than 100 meters, there's no need to add superfluous details that would be lost in the distance. The flip side is also true: if the character will be in closeup, make sure that you add convincing detail.

### How Big or Small Is the Character Relative to Other Characters?

Larger characters may need more polygons. They may need much more detailed texture maps, too. A model of an insect character would be approached differently than one of an elephant.

### Will the Character Be Animated?

A stationary character will have different needs than one that animates. For example, if the character will be standing stationary as a guard at the gate of a palace, then you will not need to be very concerned with how the joints would work. If your character will be animated, you must take much greater care when designing how things will bend and articulate.

### How Many Angles Will the Character Be Viewed From?

If you are designing a character for print, you have only one viewing angle at a time. A side-scrolling game will have only one viewing angle at a time but may have multiple views used at different locations throughout the game. A movie or real-time 3D game character will need to be viewed from all angles.

### How Much Movement Will the Character Have?

A character that will move only its arms, for example, may need more careful design than a stationary character. A completely mobile character will require a different design than a partially mobile one.

### How Fast or Slow Will the Character Be Moving?

Don't assume that because a character moves it will have to be more complicated and detailed than a stationary one. As the character's speed increases, you will reach a point of diminishing returns as far as detail and geometry because a very fast-moving character may be viewed as mostly a blur and may need a very simple design.

### Will the Character Be Close Enough to See Facial Expressions?

You will have to know if you need geometry to represent facial features or if a texture map will be enough in the final product. Obviously, if the character's expressions will be important to the role the character is to play, you must include additional detail in both the texture maps and in the geometry to be able to convey a convincing expression.

### Will the Character Need to Speak?

A character that speaks will have different geometry requirements than a silent one. A character that speaks will need a mouth that articulates and moves. This requires additional geometry in the model. The person that will be modeling the character will need a clear picture of what is expected and needed.

### How Much Detail Will You Need in the Hands, Feet, Hoofs, Talons, Paws, Etc.?

There was a time in the not-too-distant past when hands were represented by blocks of geometry with painted texture maps. Characters that held items in their hands were often modeled with the item as an integral part of the hand. Now we are seeing characters with articulating appendages. You need to know if your character will be realistic, stylized, surreal, abstract, or something completely out of left field.

### Will the Character Be Simple or Complex?

This depends completely on the end use. The only exception would be when your design may be much more detailed than the end use justifies because of potential multiple uses. An example is when the character that you are designing for a game will also be used in print advertising. While the game character would need to be somewhat simple, the print character could be more detailed and complicated.

### Who Does the Character Need to Appeal to Visually?

Know your audience and design the character appropriately. The character you are designing for a target audience consisting of teenage boys would be entirely different than a character that is designed for toddlers or an elderly audience.

### Can the Character Stand on Its Own Design If Taken out of Its Environment?

You need to check that your design would be understandable if you showed it to someone without any of the surrounding environment. For example, if you are designing a villain, could you take that villain, put it into another context, and still tell that the character is evil? If you could, then your design is working.

### Is the Character's Silhouette or Profile Readable on Its Own?

A character with a strong and recognizable silhouette will be visually stronger, more understandable, and more appealing than one whose silhouette isn't. If your character is casting a shadow on a wall, does that shadow enhance the perception of the character? If it does, then the silhouette is enhancing the look of the design.

### Will the Character Be Polygonal or Single Mesh?

There are different ways that the modeler will build a character in various 3D applications, depending on the need. Polygonal models will have seams at the joints and will call for a different treatment than a character created using a single mesh for the entire figure. You should discuss with the modeler and animator which type of model will be used. To a large degree, this will be determined by the final use of the character.

### How Do You Simplify the Character Design to Work Within the Platform's Constraints?

Until recently, it was useless to design a game character with flowing clothing or hair. The game platforms simply couldn't render the character in real time, or the time and cost required to animate the cloth for pre-rendered characters was prohibitive. Simplifying a character design is not really that hard. The main thing to remember is to work from the general to the specific. If you need to simplify a great but very complicated character design, look for the most basic general shapes that make up the character. Use the basic shape that remains as the basis of your simplification process.

### How Will the Character Animate?

If the character will animate, definitely make sure that you get some information from the animation department about what is needed and expected so your design will conform to the specifications properly.

### Do You Really Need to Remember All of This?

Unfortunately, yes, you really are expected to remember all of these issues each time you design a character. Other issues will no doubt arise with each character-design project. These are critical parts of the process.

It is important that these questions be your constant and conscious companions as you design your characters. Eventually they will become second nature and you will not be aware that you are answering them as you design; rather, their influence will always show in the underlying structure of your designs.

## CONCLUSION

In the next chapters, we will go beyond the practical and define a working method that is successful, and then we will begin to look at the magic in character design. We will specifically look at where successful ideas come from and what you can do to help yourself generate the most creative ideas possible.

# 2

# DEVELOPING A WORKING METHOD

This chapter is about the importance of developing a "working method," a series of steps you use to help organize the way you get a job done. You can benefit from defining a working method for every task that you may be asked to accomplish. Character design is no exception. If you are paddling a canoe without direction and a method, you may end up paddling in a circle and never get anywhere. So it is with character design. If you randomly scribble and draw your ideas without direction, you will never get anywhere.

This chapter presents various ideas that will help you succeed when you are assigned a character design as a job or for your own enjoyment. These ideas are by no means the only way or necessarily the right way of doing things. This working method is simply one approach to achieving successful results. It is hoped that you will be able to take what you read and apply the method with your own vision and adjustments, or vary the methods to suit your own individual goals.

## THE NEED FOR A METHODICAL AND SUCCESSFUL WAY OF WORKING

For some reason, artists tend to jump right into tasks where we are expected to draw and paint without having any sort of plan. This is because we love to sketch and draw so very much that everything else simply isn't worth worrying about. We sketch, draw, and often flounder around trying to come up with an idea. Occasionally we get lucky and come up with something useful. More often than not, we end up with an idea that may or may not be the best along with a trash can of dead ends.

There is a better way. Having a specific plan of how to approach the work will not only increase your productivity but will also lower your level of frustration. The following tasks, if you follow them in an orderly progression, will help you organize your thoughts and ideas. Then it will be easier to draw and paint a cohesive form as well as objectively gauge the success of your effort.

### 1. Identifying and Understanding the Problem

The first and most important thing to do when trying to solve any problem is to identify and understand the problem at hand. While that may sound obvious, most of us are sometimes guilty of rushing headfirst into the unknown ill prepared. Here we'll assume that your job is to design some sort of character. It does not matter who the character is for; if you don't clearly know what you're trying to accomplish, you will not be successful.

The first and sometimes hardest task to accomplish when you're identifying the problem is to make sure that both client and artist are visualizing the same thing. When a client and artist are discussing ideas, their different backgrounds can be a major obstacle to visually understanding what is needed in a character. Everyone perceives the world somewhat differently. Everything that we have experienced, been told, observed, or felt as children will affect how we view the world around us and, consequently, the images we create. If two people hear identical words or see identical images, they will not form mental images that are also identical. So it's very important to ensure that both parties understand exactly what the artist is being asked to do both visually and technically.

A typical scenario that an artist will face as a character designer might be the following:

1. The initial meeting between Sally, the artist, and Mr. Smith, the client, is going well, and both parties are excited about the scope of the project. The client tells Sally that he requires a great big, hairy, ugly villain who will pound the hero to a mushy pulp. He even uses hand gestures and sound effects to impress upon her the "badness" of the villain. Sally can see it now in her mind, and she has a clear picture of the direction that she will take with the character.
2. Once back at the studio, Sally starts drawing immediately, and the results are fantastic. This is quite possibly the finest sketch she has ever produced in such a limited amount of time, and she cannot wait to take it to Mr. Smith.
3. At the next meeting, she hands her sketch to the client with great expectation of being told that this is the finest villain ever drawn.
4. Mr. Smith's reaction is not what Sally expects; he casually tosses the sketch on the desk and tells her to try again. The rest of the meeting is a blur as she tries to figure out what happened and where she went wrong.

The problem in this scenario is that while the artist thought she understood the problem, in reality she did not clearly comprehend what was being asked of her. The client asked for several things. He wanted a villain that was big, ugly, and hairy. What did he mean when he said "big"? How many different interpretations can there be of the word "big"? What big means to one person may be entirely different than what it means to another.

When presented with such a description, an artist must find out exactly what is meant. For example, the character is big in relationship to what? The hero, an elephant, a mouse, or what exactly? The villain is big in what way? Is he tall? Muscular but not large in size? Fat or something else?

Can you see the problem? It's easy to see the same problem with the other descriptive words. What is meant by "ugly" and "hairy"? You can almost be certain that Sally's understanding is not the same as the client's.

So, how does an artist identify the problem so that everyone involved has the same understanding of what is being described? It is really very simple. Ask lots of questions. When you are told to make a character "big," respond with something like this: "You mean as big as an elephant?" Quite quickly, both you and the client will start to arrive at a shared vision.

When you have arrived back at your studio or desk, it is a very good idea to follow up the conversation with a written recap of the discussion. Write a memo or letter stating, "As per our discussion, this is what I understand you to be looking for in the character design." Be very specific in your memo. If the response is that yes, you understand exactly what is wanted, you're ready to go to the next step.

## 2. Analyzing the Problem and Breaking It Down into Simpler Elements

When you initially analyze the problem or end goal, you will look at the whole and start breaking it into manageable sections that are easily resolved. Most of these manageable sections are questions that you must answer before proceeding with the design phase.

### Coming Up with Ideas to Solve the Problem

For the majority of artists, this is one of the best parts of the whole character design process. The process of generating ideas is a combination of the visual, mental, and written. Without good ideas, you have nothing.

When you have solved all of the smaller problems, combine their solutions into larger ideas that all will solve the original problem. You should be able to come up with several different but acceptable solutions. The differences between the solutions may seem small and hardly significant, yet the more ideas you come up with, the greater your chance of hitting on a good idea.

## 3. Choosing the Best Idea

This is the tricky part. How do you tell what the best idea is? To a large degree, you will know simply by looking at your work. Some of your ideas will obviously be bad, and they will be easy to spot. After you have picked a few of the best, turn to a fresh eye so that you can narrow down the field of potential solutions. A coworker, friend, or even the art director will have a fresh perspective and should be able to give you good advice. Make sure that whoever you turn to will not patronize you and say how wonderful all of the ideas are; rather, you want that person to give you a true critique of how well the individual ideas have solved the problem.

Remember that the first idea is not usually the best; it is usually the most obvious one. Yet, if after much work, the first idea still seems to be the best, do not hesitate to go back to it.

### 4. Drawing the Character

This *is* the best part. Most artists find that there is nothing better than sitting down and drawing the day away. This is the reward for all of your hard preliminary work, and if you have successfully followed the first steps outlined earlier, you will know right where to go with the drawing.

### 5. Evaluating the Results

If all goes well, here is where you get the compliments and inflated ego. Your work will be loved, appreciated, and pivotal to the success of the project. If things do not go as well, don't be disheartened; sometimes the magic works and sometimes it doesn't. This final evaluation of your work is often the hardest part.

Have no doubt that the client will evaluate if you succeeded. Do not be afraid of failure, and do not take failure personally. You will succeed and you will fail at various times and on various projects. If what you have done does not work, go back to step one and start again. As the old saying goes, "Success is 90 percent perspiration and 10 percent inspiration."

## CONCLUSION

Trying to acquire good working habits from the very beginning of your career is very important to your long-term success. Use this suggested format or one of your own. Just make sure that all of the following steps appear somewhere in the process:

1. Identify precisely what the expectations for the character are. You must define the problem.
2. Analyze and simplify the defined problem into smaller, more manageable, problems. Come up with ideas to solve your problems. When the small questions have been answered, combine the answers to solve the large problem.
3. Choose the best character ideas that you have developed.
4. Draw the character.
5. Look at your resulting drawings. Have others look at your results. Realistically evaluate what you have done.

If you follow these five steps (or some modification of their basic premises), you will almost be guaranteed success as you design your characters. In the next chapter, we will discuss specific ideas and methods for coming up with ideas for your characters or improving ideas that you may already have.

# Expanding on Your Ideas When Creating the Character

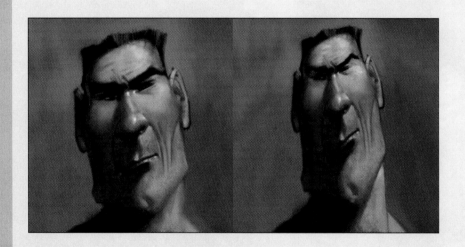

This chapter is about ideas—where they come from and how to develop the ones you have. There is no doubt that coming up with creative ideas is tough work. Nothing grows in a vacuum, and the best ideas and designs do not come easy. Artists often sit around in our studios or at our desks, virtually a vacuum, pondering where the next idea will come from. Often we sit and scribble on whatever paper is handy, tap the pencil, scribble some more, and then wonder where we lost our ability to think of good ideas.

Good character designs do not usually come from sitting, tapping a pencil, or jumping directly to the sketching. Planning and preliminary work are always needed and will pay great dividends in the finished design. This is what this chapter is all about. Here we present a few strategies to help charge your creative energy. These ideas are not the only things that you can do, but if you're stuck, they'll help get you rolling.

The majority of the exercises and suggestions presented in this chapter are about generating creative thought. While you need nothing more than your brain to give these ideas a try, you should probably have a pencil and paper ready in anticipation of that epiphany moment.

## BASIC STRATEGIES TO HELP GENERATE CREATIVE IDEAS

Coming up with new and creative ideas for a character is, at best, a lot of work. It's harder to get inspired design ideas if you simply bounce them around in the confines of your mind. If possible, get all of your senses involved.

### Learning to Relax

The first and most important thing you can do for yourself when you are faced with a creative problem is to take a deep breath and relax. Talk to yourself a little about the problem. Take another deep breath and make sure you are feeling calm and confident. The more you can lower your stress and anxiety levels, the better your chances for mental clarity will be as you begin coming up with ideas.

When you are calm, collected, and ready to start working on some great ideas, use a combination of the following suggestions to help you come up with creative ideas:

1. **Take a walk and clear your mind.** We're not talking a power walk, where you try to get exercise; we mean a stroll, during which you observe what is around you and your mind can wander. Daydream. Lie down on a grassy hill and look at the clouds. See the shapes within them and let the shapes you see suggest images to you.

Sit down on a rock by a stream or river and watch the water. All of these things will help free your mind.

2. **Closely observe the people around you every day.** If you do this, you will begin to notice special qualities that you didn't see before. As your mind begins thinking about your basic character idea, consider applying to your character the individual qualities, traits, physical appearance, quirks, habits, and faults of your friends. Don't just limit yourself to friends. Include the larger circle of your acquaintances as well as celebrities, politicians, sports stars, and anyone in the public eye. If you are designing a villain, why not base the character on people that you just do not like? You can also look at fictional characters, but watching them is not as much fun as observing real people. Remember that a fictional character is already someone else's vision and as such is nothing more than a shallow representation of a personality, whereas real people have so much more depth.

3. **Have a brainstorming session with a few other people.** Brainstorming by yourself is never successful, but brainstorm with four or five people and see what happens. As an example of how well this works, try to think of 50 new and unique ways to use a brick. If you did this exercise alone, you probably couldn't come up with 50 variations. But if you get four or five creative people together in a room, they will likely come up with some very creative ideas. Of course, many of the ideas will not be usable. Usability is not the point, and it does not matter if some of the ideas are outrageous. The point is to begin looking at the subject in a new light. Figure 3.1 shows what it can sometimes feel like when you have to come up with new ideas.

## Locating Useful Reference Materials

Being able to find appropriate reference materials and learning how to use them is one of the most important abilities an artist can have. In fact, one of the most important skills you can acquire is knowing how to find information that will be useful and inspiring to you as you design your character. Learn how to use the local library. Learn how to use the Internet to find visually inspiring imagery; you can find anything on the Internet these days. The vast amount of visual and written information on the Web can be overwhelming if you are not careful, so make sure to spend your time effectively.

## Using Wordplay

Playing with words can be one of the best ways to come up with good ideas. Basically, this exercise consists of writing columns of words and combining them in unusual ways. You can literally draw lines from one

**FIGURE 3.1**    Brainstorming can be painful but rewarding.

word to another. Combinations you never thought of will arise. If needed, take some time to create lists that are specific to the project you are working on. It would not do much good to list ocean creatures if you were working on a space character.

Here is an example of a very short list to illustrate the concept of combining words to form new ideas to work with. Of course, this list is not meant for any specific problem; the lists that you would use should be customized to your problem. Of course, some combinations work better than others. A "sharp heroic" does not make much sense.

Knight
Obtuse
Shiny

Vicious
Mermaid
Heroic
King
Warthog
Sharp
Friendly
Monster
Ostrich

## Fantasizing About the Character

Fantasize about the character that you need to design. Fantasizing goes hand in hand with both brainstorming and daydreaming. Fantasizing is more an individual activity where you would imagine "what if"-type situations about your character, whereas brainstorming is best in a group setting, as we have seen. When fantasizing, you will want to get out of the everyday modes of thought and see how far out you can take your ideas. "What if?" is the biggest question to ask yourself when you fantasize.

## Using Symbolism with the Character

Give the character personality or traits that have symbolic elements. Many symbolic elements are very easy to relate with. If you use appropriate symbols, your audience will get quick clues to a character's personality. For example, if a halo is put over a character's head, assumptions can be made, whether right or wrong, about the character. The symbolism may be public and easily recognized by many people. Or, it may be private and have meaning only to you, the creator. Many books that list different symbols and their meanings are available. Some symbols are timeless while others are more contemporary. Examples of some things with symbolic meaning are white doves, bats, black cats, gold, lead, the planets, and astrological symbols.

## Building the Character Around a Myth

Build your character around a myth; or, create a myth around your character. Mythologize your character. The human race has so many different myths and legends that it's easy—and to a degree smart—to use them as a basis for your characters because a mythical character's history is already so well defined. The character Dracula has become such a strong cultural symbol of the myth that designing a "new" Dracula would take a lot of work to break the visual mold.

## Snowballing

Just as a snowball gains size and speed as it rolls down a hill, snowballing an idea can help it gain momentum and size. Snowballing is simply adding more and more wacky notions to a developing idea. Use snowballing in conjunction with brainstorming, fantasy, wordplay, or just about any other idea-creating exercise.

## Visiting Special Places for Inspiration

Visit the zoo. Some of the best ideas can come when you watch the animals as well as the people. Figure 3.2 shows an unusual character based on someone seen at the zoo. Along these same lines, go and spend the

**FIGURE 3.2**    An interesting character seen at the local zoo.

day at the local airport with a sketchbook. You will be amazed by the amount of inspiration that walks by.

## DEVELOPING YOUR BASIC IDEA

Getting the basic idea of a character is always the hardest part of the creative process. By doing the simple things we discussed in the last section and not just sitting at your desk in the dark trying to be inspired, you will open up new avenues of experience that can lead to new ideas for your characters. However, the basic idea is only the first step. You now have a vision, but it is only a somewhat ghostlike visage on the edge of your conscience. Your basic idea is floating around either in your mind or on paper. You know where you want to go with this idea, but you're feeling somewhat lost as to a direction.

The strategies in the previous section are mostly cerebral, whereas the methods discussed here are best done visually with a piece of paper and pencil. Not only will you have a record of idea changes, but your drawings will also help to generate additional ideas. Use relatively inexpensive paper and a soft pencil, marker, or pen.

Do not erase! This is very important. You are not drawing pretty pictures but generating differing ideas. An eraser will slow you down and kill the creative flow. No one else is meant to see the images you will create; they are just your thought processes and ideas coming to life. Don't expect them to look solid and refined at this point.

The following are some strategies to help you develop a basic but vague idea into a more concrete visual image ready to be drawn or sketched. They are not the only ways to firm up an idea but are good methods for continuing the process. As noted in the previous section, use these ideas in conjunction with each other.

### Using Caricature

You can caricature just about anything you are drawing: people, animals, plants, and maybe even rocks. Caricature can be used to further develop ideas that seem to have gone stale. Quite often, caricature, while humorous, is looking for the essence of the subject. If you are having trouble seeing where to go with a design, try doing a caricature of what you already have. Once you have again found the essence of the caricature, continue with the design. Figure 3.3 shows an example of caricature.

**FIGURE 3.3**  A caricature of a family dog.

## Using Humor

Humor is a great way to take an idea that is stalled and jump-start the creative process. Humor's main purpose is to entertain and generally does not need a lot of explanation. Humor does not try to make a statement. For example, if you are developing a serious barbarian character, put him in a humorous situation or change his props to something humorous (as in Figure 3.4), and see how many more creative vistas open for you.

## Using Blotter Pictures

So you are still stuck. You still need to design new and exciting characters and even costumes for them. Perhaps you should try using some blotter pictures to get some ideas brewing. Blotter pictures are the same thing as the famous Rorschach psychological test and are extremely easy to do on the computer. Figure 3.5 shows an example of a blotter picture.

Black and white as well as color work well. Black and white usually works better when you are trying to come up with ideas for form shapes (Figure 3.6), whereas color tends to work better for ideas that are decorative in nature (Figure 3.7).

**FIGURE 3.4**    A gladiator armed only with asparagus and a smile.

**FIGURE 3.5**    A computer-generated inkblot.

**FIGURE 3.6**    A black and white inkblot picture.

**FIGURE 3.7**    A color inkblot picture.

## Using Exaggeration

Exaggeration, which is an integral part of caricature, is fairly self-explanatory. Take your character idea and exaggerate some portion of it. The exaggeration can either be extreme or subtle, depending on your intention. Be careful that you do not exaggerate everything within the character. After all, exaggeration is based on the difference between things that we consider the norm and things that are not the norm. Figure 3.8 shows an already exaggerated face that has been exaggerated even more.

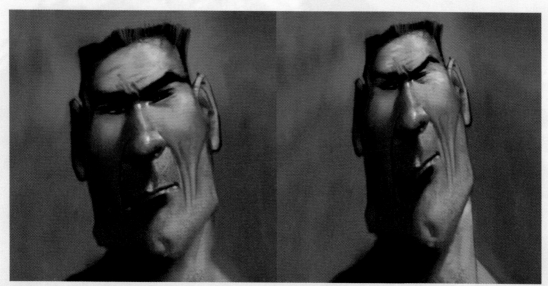

**FIGURE 3.8**   An exaggerated character.

### Using Satire

Satire is humor but with teeth. The teeth can be large and very sharp, or small and relatively painless. Humor becomes satire when it begins to deliver a message. The humor in satire is almost always aggressive and critical with the purpose of entertaining or scolding while delivering its message. Political cartoonists are experts at using satire with a character.

### Using Parody

Parody is one step beyond satire and needs the viewer's knowledge of the subject to work. Parody can simply entertain like humor, try to educate or scold like satire, or try to do both. For the parody to work, the audience must be familiar with the original subject and be able to see the similarities between both the original and the changed version. For example, a fat little Dracula-type character dressed in white would be a parody of the classic version we are all familiar with.

### Doing Some Expression Exercises

So every character that you draw has the facial expression of a zombie. No wonder the characters lack life. Every character needs to have expression, and the majority of that expression is found in the face and body language. A good way to practice drawing facial expressions is to revert to the most basic elements that drive an expression: the eyes, nose, and mouth. As quickly as possible, draw a series of expressions using only lines for the facial features. Some of them will be garbage but some will look like something. Take the ones that look like something and develop them further.

## Doing Some Five-Dot Action Exercises

Similar to expression exercises, five-dot action exercises help the artist get out of the doldrums of static character poses. The exercise is simple to set up but harder to complete. Take a dozen or so pieces of paper and have a coworker draw five dots on each. Each page of dots should be different. It really does not matter if the dots are in some sort of order or completely random. When you have the paper back, draw your character on each page using four of the dots to represent each individual hand and foot; the fifth dot will represent the head. If your character is not a quadruped, include additional dots as required.

## Using Folded Paper

This exercise usually allows you to come up with some very interesting results. Three or four artists each draw a section of a character on a folded piece of paper. No artist can see the previous artist's work, save for the lower eighth of an inch or so of the previous drawing. Taking that small section and knowing what part of the character the artist is expected to draw, each artist completes the assigned section, folds the page so that only the bottom bit is showing, and passes it to the next artist. Several iterations of this exercise can often lead to extraordinary images and ideas.

## Using Idealization

The concept is as simple as it sounds. Take your character idea and make it the ideal of whatever it is. Knowing what the ideal of a character is makes it easier to make a realistically flawed character.

## Adding and Subtracting

Just like in math, you can add and subtract parts of the character. First, you can try adding things to the design, such as actual body parts, a costume, or some equipment. Then, do the reverse. Take your character and begin removing things—body parts or accessories; it does not matter. The method is simply to get you to look at things differently.

## Using Repetition

Somewhat similar to the technique of adding and subtracting is using repetition. Take an element of the design and repeat it numerous times. Once again, do not be limited by your imagination; rather, let your imagination run wild.

## Using Combinations

Combining differing elements has always been one of the sparks that fires an artist's imagination. Who would have thought to combine a horse with a human? Combine any number of differing elements and see what is possible. This strategy is similar to the wordplay method we discussed earlier in this chapter in that you are combining ideas. If it helps, write down the different things that you are considering combining and make choices from the list. Combine organic and inorganic elements. Combine geometric and organic shapes.

## Transferring Characteristics

Try transferring the characteristics from one object to another. This is a simple concept. Transfer characteristics from an inorganic object to an organic one. Or try transferring the characteristics from something mechanical to a plant. Transferring characteristics is about transferring the physical as well as the not-so-physical attributes between objects and characters.

## Superimposing

Superimposing is similar to combining characters or objects except that instead of mixing two separate objects together, you are superimposing one over the other. This can be done at more than one level. Again, you are encouraged to try things that you normally would not consider doing.

## Changing the Scale

Take a part of your idea and change the scale. Change the scale of your whole character if it will work. To effectively change the scale of an object, you must include something within the image or on the character to give a visual clue as to the scale. Making a character a giant does not work unless something around the character gives visual clues to the imposing size. The reverse is also true if you are making a diminutive character.

### Substituting

Substitute a portion or prop of your character with something different. Perhaps even substitute something really different. Make that sword a paintbrush or vice versa.

### Distorting

Distortion is very self-explanatory. Shear, twist, fold, spindle, and mutilate your character, portions of your character, the original idea, the costume, anything. Nothing is sacred and beyond your ability to distort.

### Disguising the Character

Change the appearance of your character with disguise. Possibly all you need to add is something as simple as sunglasses. Or maybe sometimes you need something more extreme, such as sunglasses with a fake nose and a mustache.

### Using Analogy

Take two of your character designs and create an analogy between them. Take different characters and make something about them similar. For example, how could you make a weight lifter and ballerina seem more similar? Could you add a tutu to the weight lifter? Could you add something else? As you see what the results are, continue with differing and additional characters.

### Creating a Hybrid

Create a hybrid by taking two of your characters and imagining that they produce offspring. What would happen if one of the characters were a robot and the other were a plant? No combination is too outrageous.

### Evolving the Character

Evolution is a very subtle process, with change being gradual and sometimes hardly visible. Evolving a character can be one of the most fun and rewarding ways of creating new and exciting characters. Simply pick something about your character design and modify it slightly. Take this changed character and then alter the changed element slightly. Continue with this type of progression as long as you like.

## Changing the Character with Metamorphosis and Mutation

The opposite of evolving a character is to metamorphose or mutate that character. Metamorphoses and mutations are dramatic changes. A most common example of a metamorphosis would be how a caterpillar changes into a butterfly. Metamorphoses are generally caused by some internal action. On the other hand, the dramatic changes that are the result of a mutation are generally caused by an outside influence. Taking your character design and metamorphosing or mutating it into a different character is risky. There is a good chance that you will lose the original idea if not careful.

## Using Metaphors

A metaphor is a figure of speech where a word or phrase that usually means one thing is used to describe another; in a sense, you are comparing the two things. You can use this to great advantage when designing similar yet different characters.

## Using Visual Puns

A pun is when you play with similar-sounding words that have different meanings, or different-meaning words with the same sound. The visual equivalent of a pun can be a good way of generating new and creative ideas. Good sources for visual puns are cliché sayings.

## Doodling and Scribbling

Just sitting down and beginning to scribble and doodle is a great way to expand on an idea that is just forming. Doodles and scribbles should be quickly executed with little detail until the idea begins to solidify.

## Making Things Look Strange, or Transforming the Ordinary into the Fantastic

As you develop your character idea, take some of the idea and see how strange you can make the figure look while still being recognizable. This technique works very well for a character's props and costumes. In general, the more you can push an idea, the better the ideas you come up with will be.

## Using Mimicry

Mimicry is a technique of deception that is very common in the animal world. Many harmless creatures will take on the physical attributes of other, more dangerous, creatures. This has the direct benefit of scaring off predators. This is the opposite of camouflage, as the mimic generally wants to be noticeable and advertise its deceptive danger. Though this is not generally a good method of character design because of the tendency to confuse the audience, it is nevertheless a great way of generating new ideas.

## CONCLUSION

Chapter 2 suggested some activities that could help you begin to formulate ideas when presented with the challenge of designing characters. This chapter described a number of rather specific ideas that can help you expand on a very basic idea you've already developed. From here on in, the book will now assume that you now have a pretty solid idea of where your character design is headed. The next chapters will help you create the finished products. First, we will start by creating the character's history. From there, we will explore the personality and physical look of the character.

# MAKING THE CHARACTER REAL BY CREATING A CHARACTER HISTORY

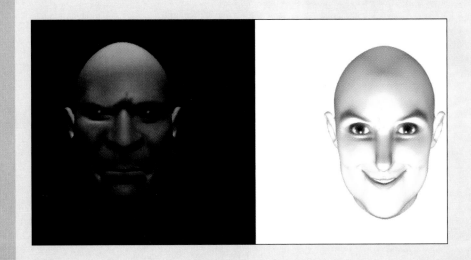

C hapters 1 through 3 were about coming up with ideas. This chapter expands on your ideas so you can actually design the character's look. By now you should have some basic ideas about your character and possibly a few sketches. The image of your character is becoming clearer, and for the most part you are feeling pretty good about your design. Now is the time to think about the history and look of the character.

This chapter is about making your character real and about communicating aspects of the character to others. Doing so allows you to help the modelers and animators see the character as real as possible. It will also help you, the designer, put the finishing touches on your character.

## CREATING THE CHARACTER'S HISTORY

You may be wondering what the point of having a character history is. The character you are designing is only for a video game, after all, and not an epic novel. Well, a character history helps you, the designer, truly get to know what you are going to be drawing. Having a history for your character helps you pose the small questions that will give you the insight needed to make a successful design.

The steps to creating a character's history are simple and involve no more than answering a few questions. Be sure to write the history down as either a list or simple, descriptive paragraphs.

The next few sections cover the things you should consider when thinking about what your character's history will be.

### The Character's Past, Present, and Future

Just as your friends and acquaintances are much more interesting when you know something about them, your character will be more interesting to the audience when something more is known about it. Consider the following about your character:

**The character's past.** Where is your character from and what were the character's formative years or youth like? Has the character had a very mobile past, or was the character born and raised in one area? Your character may not always have a distant past; maybe your character is only a week old and the past is not an issue.

**The character's present situation.** What has been happening with and to your character within the past few days, weeks, or months? Where is the character cu35rrently living and why?

**The character's future.** Isn't it wonderful that you are psychic and can see the future of your character? Use this information to help you develop the character's present.

## The Character's Everyday Environment

The question of environment is an important one. Quite often, the environment that a character lives in will to a large degree determine the general physical look of your creation. Consider the following:

- Where is the character from? What specific environment did your character originate in?
- Where does the character live now?
  - Outer space? Will the character need a space suit to operate in our typical earth environment?
  - Aquatic? Will the character be slimy and breathe through gills?
  - Subterranean? Will the character have large digging claws and no eyes?
  - Airborne? Will the character be light as a feather or winged?
  - Surface dweller? Will the character resemble a human?
  - Some exotic environment? Will the character be a methane breather that drinks ammonia?
  - A combination? Will the character be some combination of the above?

Considering where your character is from will help you arrive at a general physical look very quickly. From that point, you can experiment to your heart's desire as far as the small touches.

## The Character's Personality

If you answer the following questions, you will begin to get a good feel of what a character's personality will be based on. Once you have the reasons for the way a character should behave, you may then figure out how that character will actually act. Here are the questions to ask:

- What is your character's personality and how has your character's history affected that personality?
- What is the character's name? This sounds obvious, but you would be surprised how many characters don't have a name.
- What is the character's family tree?
- Is the character based on legend or myth? If the character is based on one, will the audience know and understand the origin of the legend or myth?
- Is the character based on another's work? If so, is the author living or deceased? Will you have any licensing issues if the character is too recognizable?
- Was the character born, created, or hatched?
- What is the character's body language and how does that help define the personality? Subconsciously, we all read each other's body

language. Make sure that your character's body language fits the character's personality, profession, or gender.

- Was the character's family life good, bad, neutral, or nonexistent?
- Is the character educated or illiterate? An educated caveman will behave entirely different than an uneducated caveman. Likewise, an educated caveman will be different than an educated astronaut. Make sure the education is appropriate to the character.
- What are the character's current living conditions? Is the character obsessively or compulsively neat, or is slob a more apt description? Are the character's living conditions advanced or primitive?
- Does the character have a job, trade, or commercial skill? Though this may not directly affect the look or feel of a character, it may. A lumberjack assassin will look different than a ballet dancer assassin.
- Does the character need a commercial skill? Again, this may or may not affect your character design.
- Does the character have or need a financial status? A rich character may be able to outfit itself better than a poor one. A rich character will possibly be able to hire others to do his bidding.
- What are the character's favorite foods?
- Does the character have any favorite activities, hobbies, etc.?

## The Character's Personality Traits

It is so very important to get to know your character. If you answer these simple questions when you are laying the foundation for your design, your design will be believable and living to the audience:

- Is the character slow to anger or constantly in a rage?
- Is the character shy or bold?
- Is the character greedy or generous?
- Is the character sneaky or gullible?
- Is the character superstitious?
- How romantic is the character?
- Does the character have any personality quirks such as twitches, psychoses, or phobias?
- What, if any, are the character's defining moments?
- Has the character had any triumphs or failures?
- How does the character treat others?
- What are the character's politics?
- Is the character religious?
- Does the character own property?
- Does the character have servants, pets, a harem, etc.?
- Does the character have any unusual mental or physical characteristics?
- What are the character's day-to-day activities?
- Is your character a couch potato or a soldier?

### The Character's Look

Once you know your character's personality, it is just as important to know his or her look. Ask yourself the following questions to help refine your mental image of the character:

- How technically advanced is the character? Is he a caveman, space jockey, or bottom-dwelling scum sucker?
- What are the character's defensive capabilities?
- What are the character's offensive capabilities?
- Does the character wear clothing, armor, or costumes?
- Does the character have style and, if so, what is that style like?
- What are the audience's expectations for the character? What does the audience expect visually? How does the audience expect the character to act?

## CONCLUSION

If you can answer all the questions mentioned in this chapter, you will "know" your creation, which is vital to a good design. In the next chapter, we will go over some basic questions to ask yourself so that you can finalize the physical look of the character.

# 5

# DESIGNING THE PHYSICAL LOOK OF YOUR CHARACTER

By this point in the design process, you probably have a pretty good idea of what your character is going to look like. This chapter gives you some questions to ask yourself as you are refining your mental image of the character. For the most part, you can use this chapter as an outline of things to consider when you begin drawing the character. For these exercises, you just need some paper and a few sharp pencils.

## DESCRIBING THE CHARACTER

So what does your character look like? By this time, you probably have a vague mental image of what your character will look like, but can you describe the look to the audience? This section will help you develop that mental image into a specific look for your character.

### The Character's General Physical Characteristics

Here are some general aspects of the character to consider:

- What is the character's general physiology and body makeup?
- If the character has legs, how many are there? Is your character a biped or a quadruped, or does the character have more than four legs?
- Is your character animal like? What kind of animal does it resemble? Is it like a mammal, bird, reptile, amphibian, fish, insect, some lower form of life, or something else entirely that is alive only in your mind?
- How many appendages besides legs does the character have?
- How many heads are there? Does one dominate, or do all of them think and react alike?
- How many arms are there, and where are they positioned?
- Does your character have wings? If so, what kind? Are they like those of a bat, bird, or insect? Are they fin-like?
- Does your character have a tail? Does it have more than one, and where are the tails located?
- Is anything extra attached to the character?
- How and what does the character eat? Is the character a carnivore and kind of scary, or a mild-mannered and gentle herbivore? Is the character an omnivore or insectivore?

### The Character's Body Type

You need to decide if the character will have one of the three kinds of body types, or if the character is something else entirely. The three body types are as follows:

**Ectomorph.** Those with this body type have the following characteristics:

- Are thin
- Have small bones
- Have a flat chest
- Are delicately built
- Are young and youthful in appearance
- Are tall
- Are lightly muscled
- Have stooped shoulders
- Have a large brain
- Have difficulty gaining weight
- Take longer to grow muscles
- Have a short upper body
- Have long arms and legs
- Have long and narrow feet and hands
- Have very little body fat
- Have a narrow chest and narrow shoulders as well as long, thin muscles
- Have a high metabolism

**Endomorph.** Those with this body type have the following characteristics:

- Have a soft body
- Have large bones
- Have a slow metabolism
- Have underdeveloped muscles as well as a small amount of muscle mass and small muscles
- Have a round-shaped body
- Have an overdeveloped digestive system
- Have trouble losing weight
- Generally find it easy to build muscle
- Have short musculature
- Have a round face
- Have a short neck
- Have wide hips
- Have a high body fat percentage

**Mesomorph.** Those with this body type have the following characteristics:

- Have a hard, muscular body
- Have medium-sized to large bones
- Have a medium to high metabolism
- Have an overly mature appearance
- Have a rectangular-shaped body

- Have thick skin
- Have a low to medium body fat percentage
- Have a large amount of muscle mass and large muscles
- Have an upright posture
- Gain or lose weight easily
- Grow muscle quickly
- Have a large chest
- Have a long torso
- Are very strong

Within the body types, there are other things to consider, such as the body style. Is the character fat, skinny, buff, or a combination of different body styles?

## The Character's Proportions

Here are some things to consider about the character's proportions:

- Is the character built like a superhero, an ordinary guy, or a 98-pound weakling?
- How does the environment affect the character's proportions? A character from a high-gravity environment, for example, will be very different from a character from a low-gravity environment. You also need to think about the effect of temperature extremes on the character's proportions.

## The Character's Makeup

You need to consider what the character is made of. Your character could be made of any of the following or a combination thereof:

- Flesh and bones
- Plants
- Metal
- Plastic
- Stones or minerals

Or perhaps the character is ethereal, like a ghost or a flame.

## The Character's Gender

There are various characteristics to consider here:

- Is the character male, female, a hermaphrodite, or something else entirely?
- What are the primary physical differences of the genders?
- What are the secondary physical differences of the genders?

## The Character's Surface

The following are what you need to consider about the character's surface covering:

- Does the character have skin? If so, what are the color, texture, and hairiness, and are there variations from body part to body part?
- Does the character have fur? If so, what are the color, texture, and thickness, and are there variations from body part to body part? If the character has fur, does the character shed?
- Does the character have scales? If so, what are the color, texture, and thickness, and are there variations from body part to body part?
- Does the character have feathers? If so, what are the color, texture, and thickness, and are there variations from body part to body part?
- Does the character have a shell, slime, cilia, or something else entirely?

## The Character's Color

What range of colors is the character? How does the character's color affect the audience's perception of the character? Is the character able to change colors like a chameleon? Are differing parts of the character different colors? Are the character's colors used for camouflage or warning?

## The Character's Facial Structure

You need to consider the following regarding the character's face:

- What is your character's facial structure, and what are the character's facial features?
- How many faces and features are there?
- How many eyes are there? How expressive are the character's eyes?
- Does the character have breathing parts or some other breathing structure?
- Does the character have mouth parts?
- Will the character be capable of speech?
- Does the character have antennae or something else entirely?
- Where are the features placed in relation to each other?

## The Character's Movement

Here are some things to consider as far as how the character moves:

- What is the character's method of motion? Does the character fly, swim, crawl, burrow, walk upright or on all fours, squirm, or hop? Is it jet propelled like an octopus, or does it travel around on wheels?
- How does your character move when in motion?

- When the character begins to move, which body part moves first, and which moves last?
- How does the character carry its weight when in motion, and how does the character stand?
- How does the character move when idle or when nervous? What about when angry or frightened?
- Is there a particular stance or pose that defines the character's attitude about life?

## Other Considerations

If you answer the questions posed throughout this chapter, you will have a pretty concrete idea of what your character look like. Here are a few miscellaneous but important things to keep in mind when designing a character:

**Using stereotypes.**   To add a degree of familiarity to your character, you can carefully use stereotypes when appropriate and not offensive. After all, we do typically associate certain characteristics with different character types. Barbarians, for example, are not generally skinny, 98-pound weaklings.

**Fooling the audience.**   Don't try to do this. Make bad guys look like bad guys. Make the monsters threatening, for example. The audience expects a certain personality for different looks. Do not stray too far from the expected or you will confuse the audience.

**Being sensitive.**   Always remember to be sensitive and careful when you are dealing with and using cultural and symbolic elements in your creations.

**Providing scale.**   Remember to give a clue as to the scale of your character. If you create a giant, you must place something near him to give a sense of scale. Without anything to identify the scale of a character, the audience will have no idea of its size. The same character could be perceived as a giant or a midget depending on how you outfit your character and its surroundings.

**Connecting the character to reality.**   Make sure that there is some connection to reality. Your character needs to have a point of reference. If you create something that is unrecognizable, your audience will not relate to the character. It is no accident that most monsters walk and act generally like we do. We recognize the look of creatures that resemble ourselves and have expectations for how a character will generally behave.

**Being original.**   Try to balance between using kitsch and being totally original. Kitsch is something that appeals to popular or lowbrow taste and is often of poor quality. Use kitsch items sparingly when designing your character. Kitsch can add a subtle sense of humor, but if it's overdone it will look silly. Unless you have a good reason, generally try to avoid fads. They will date the character immediately. Not much is truly original anymore, but do make it a point to not blatantly copy another's works and ideas.

## The Visual Issues of Character Design and How to Communicate Your Ideas

One of the easiest ways to communicate your character ideas is by using comparison. If the character is soft and delicate, make the character round without many angles. If the character is rough and ready, the design should be made of angular shapes.

Here are some other tips:

**Working from the general to the specific.**   Doing this when designing is always well founded. If your character is understandable early on, the greater the chances of him being understandable as you move along with your design.

**Simplify when possible.**   As in just about everything in life, the simplest statements are generally the easiest to understand. You have no idea how sophisticated your audience may be, but aim for a simple design that will work with all levels of understanding

**Do not use too many little bits and pieces.**   You will only confuse your audience. Remember that the devil is in the details. Don't overdo it. You recognize your friends by their general look and not by how many freckles they have on their nose.

**Build characters out of basic shapes.**   Just about everything we see in the world around us can be built out of a few basic shapes: cubes, spheres, cones, and cylinders. Try to base your character on these basic shapes.

**Test the silhouettes of your character.**   If the silhouette visually stands on its own, the character design will be stronger.

**Maintain consistency in the character's environment.**   Variety is the spice of life, but when you are designing characters for the same environment, they should have a similar look and feel.

**Avoid repeating the same formula over and over again when designing.**   For example, do not put a beard on every character.

## CONCLUSION

Remember that being able to communicate your ideas through your character is one of the most important things that you can do as a character designer. Your character serves dual purposes, and it must fill each equally well. First are the needs of the media for which you are designing it; second, you must fulfill your own creative needs. Following the ideas presented in this and previous chapters will help you accomplish each of these goals. In the next chapter, we will take the idea you have developed and begin to explore some of the more traditional artistic principles that will help you communicate this idea effectively to your audience.

# ARTISTIC PRINCIPLES
# FOR A DIGITAL AGE

Why would a book that is dedicated to digital art contain a part on tradition artistic principles? While the argument can be made that judging art is a subjective business, there is no argument that all good art is based on very non-subjective principles.

In today's fast-paced, information-overloaded, digital age, we sometimes overlook the very basic principles and strategies that the craft of art is based on. The computer is such a powerful tool and the software that we use anticipates our needs so well that there is a tendency to let the technology do all of the work. This is why there is such a big market in program plug-ins. Click a button and, all of a sudden, the image looks like a painting. This approach of letting the computer make the decisions is simply wrong and shortsighted, if your goal is to create true digital art. It may also be the reason that there is so much hesitancy for the public to accept digital works as art, because the computer has done the work.

This is why a part of this book is dedicated to traditional principles. If you are a beginner, you may not have ever had a discussion on value and color or their uses. If you are a professional, maybe you are letting the ghost in the machine do a little too much of the work. Either way, a refresher on traditional picture-making principles is appropriate in a book on digital painting.

Go through this part and read each chapter, then in your next image try to use some of the information in your painting. Your work should definitely improve.

# Basic Principles for Improving the Drawing, Sketching, and Painting of Your Character

This chapter presents you with a few tips to help you with your figure and character work. Some of these things will sound obvious, and you have probably heard many of them before; however, some may be new to you. Your work will improve if you do them.

## SOME BASIC IDEAS ABOUT DRAWING

If you remember these simple ideas as you are drawing, you will notice a dramatic, positive change in the quality of your sketches:

**The first thing you can do to improve your figure work is to draw constantly.**    This should sound obvious and yet most of us become comfortable with a level of competence that is far below our capabilities. Though it's good to draw anything, concentrate on the figure. You need to focus on the figure because artists know intimately what the figure looks like and we should be able to easily spot our problems when drawing it. Drawing a tree is fine, but you can move a branch up or down six inches and no one will ever care. Move an arm up or down six inches, and it's guaranteed that everyone will notice. Practice drawings should be concerned with accuracy and do not have to be beautiful.

**Draw from the living figure if possible.**    Drawing from a living figure is the only way to learn to impart a sense of life in one's work. When working from life, you learn how to adapt to the small changes that you see, as the model invariably shifts and moves slightly. If drawing from life is not feasible, draw the figure from available pictures.

**When you begin a drawing, lightly place spots on the paper that will help define the outermost points of the figure.** Place a mark on your paper that corresponds with each spot of the body that extends farthest from the body's center point. These marks, if connected, will form an envelope that will encompass the entire figure and will give you a framework within which you can work.

**Always start with the general and work toward the specific.** Start by drawing the simplest shapes that you see. Make them exactly correct and then start adding the smaller shapes. If you get the big picture right, the little picture can do nothing but follow.

**Avoid drawing the eyelashes.**    Actually, avoid drawing any of the small details that really add nothing to the character and the essence of your drawing. The devil is in the details. You can recognize someone you know at a great distance not by seeing the color of her eyes but by the essence of her being. This is what you want to strive for in your work—the accurate representation of the essence of the figure.

**Make your proportions correct.**    Surprisingly, many pieces of figurative art have awful proportions. With all the available information in books, there is no excuse for not learning it. By knowing what an average human looks like, you will have a greater chance for success when distorting the figure to fill your specific needs.

**Learn your surface anatomy.**    Knowing how the muscles play out on the surface of the figure makes sketching and building models much easier with more believable results. Learning this information will also help you design nonhuman characters better.

## SOME BASIC IDEAS ABOUT PAINTING FIGURES, HAIR, AND FLESH TONES

Now we'll switch from drawing to painting. This section covers a few things for you to remember as you strive to do your best painting on your character work.

One of the most confusing aspects of painting a character is how to paint good flesh tones. Let's learn some of the secrets of painting good flesh tones.

A certain young art student wanted to know the "secret" formula for painting good flesh tones. He of course tried all the available tube mixtures, but he generally got awful results. This student finally thought he had found the secret one day when he stumbled on the oil color burnt sienna. What a great color. Burnt sienna can be mixed with white and will give you this beautiful, peachy, flesh color. Unfortunately, using this color led to unexpected results. The paintings had a boring and unrealistic feel to them. The student had not yet found the secret formula, because there is no secret formula.

The following are some hints and tips to help you "paint" your characters better:

**There are no secret formulas for flesh colors.**    Flesh color varies greatly from person to person and from different locations on the body. In traditional painting, all your flesh colors can be mixed with a red, yellow, and cool color (blue, green, black, etc.). Though you don't mix colors digitally the same way, the reasoning would be the same; you should use cooled-down pinks, oranges, and yellows.

**Generally speaking, make the flesh tones of your male characters darker than those of your female characters.**    In most ethnic ranges, you can almost always get away with slightly lighter skin for your female characters.

**The general complexion for a figure is found in the chest area.** As you move out along the figure, the flesh tones become ruddier and darker. The hands, feet, elbows, and knees are distinctly redder and darker in appearance than the skin color in the center of the chest.

**The face can be divided into three zones of color.**    From the hair line to the eyebrows is a zone of golden color. From the eyebrows to the bottom of the nose is a zone of red color. From the bottom of the nose to the bottom of the chin is a zone of blue or cooler color. These zones of colors should be played up much more in male characters than in female ones. Figure 6.1 shows these three zones.

**FIGURE 6.1**    The zones of color in the face.

**Look for highlights.**    You can find them in the following locations: the bridge and tip of the nose, the corners of the eyes, the corner where the nostrils meet the face, the upper lip, the corners of the mouth, and the chin. Highlights are almost always in these spots, with slight variations. They can act like signs on a map to help you make sure that your features are properly located. Figure 6.2 shows highlighting on the face.

**FIGURE 6.2**    The location of highlights on the face.

**Skin acts very much like a white surface in its interaction with the surrounding environment.** Skin will reflect and be affected by colors from everything around it. A figure in a red costume will have much redder skin than a figure in a blue costume.

Here are some other things to keep in mind when you are drawing a face:

- Skin almost always reflects back into itself with an orange hue.
- Make sure that you always put some of the background colors into your skin tones.
- Make sure that there is a full range of value from lights to darks within your flesh tones. (This has nothing to do with ethnic backgrounds, as you will find lights in darker-skinned people and darks in lighter-skinned individuals.)
- Dark-skinned people have shinier skin than light-skinned people do.
- The highlights on the skin always have a tint of the light's color in them.
- Fleshy areas tend to be warm, while bony areas will be cooler.

- Dark skin has more blue in it than light skin. Dark skin that has been exposed to the sun has more reddish tones than blue ones.
- Ruddy-toned skin has a lot of violet touches.
- Mid-tone skin has a lot of golden colors.
- Light skin is usually very cool.
- Stay away from using too much yellow when painting blond hair. Use lots of warm, yellowish grays and cooled brown with touches of yellow in the highlights.
- Red hair has lots of oranges and purples in the light areas.
- The highlights on black hair often appear bluish. The same is true for dark brown hair but not to the same degree.
- Use deep red colors to draw the lines between lips, nostrils, and lines between fingers, etc. Using a dark brown or black will kill the feeling of life in the art.
- Keep your colors in the flesh cooler than you think you need to.

## THE ART PART: SKETCHING, DRAWING, AND PAINTING THE CHARACTER

When you are in the sketch phase, your ideas really come to life. There are also a number of other very good reasons to develop your ideas in quick sketches:

- Sketches are quick and inexpensive. Pencils and paper are relatively cheap.
- You can revise and rework your ideas quickly.
- You can quickly progress from very basic ideas to very detailed depictions of your character.
- You can get almost immediate feedback. When you look at sketch designs, it is very easy for the client to say whether things are going in the right direction.

Depending on your mood, sketch directly on the computer or just on paper. Either way is fine.

It is usually a good idea to sketch your character from several angles and possibly with several expressions. This approach may help you catch problems with your look and feel.

Here are some things you must know and remember to do so that the character will be pleasing both to you and the audience:

- You must know what the things you are drawing look like. Therefore, the following is very important:
  - You must know anatomy, both human and animal.
  - You must know about balance and how to make sure that your character has it.

- You need to be aware of figure composition or how to display the figure in a pleasing arrangement with its surroundings.
- You need to be able to draw with both a simplicity and intensity in your work. You need simplicity so that the viewer can see the idea first; you need intensity so that the viewer can see the emotion and mood in your picture.
- You need to be able to combine your character with props and objects in an intelligent and visually pleasing fashion. The right props make your character designs effective. Bad props make for bad pictures.
- You must be able to express rhythm and motion in your character drawings. Rhythm is not the depiction of excessive action but the implied motion of the figure. Movement refers to actual depiction of motion within your drawing.
- You must be able to place emphasis where you want, and control the center of interest and the focal point of your images.

## CONCLUSION

This chapter has presented some ideas on how to make drawings and paintings of your characters easier and better looking. While these ideas are not really profound in and of themselves, as a whole they often will make a difference between a bad-to-average drawing and a good-to-excellent one. It is good practice to review these ideas periodically so that they will eventually become second nature to you. In the next chapter, we will discuss value and its use in your art. For some reason, value is an easy subject to understand, but it is hard to implement in many artists' work. It is hoped that the next chapter will give some insight into this elusive subject.

CHAPTER

# 7

# VALUE AND ITS USE IN PICTURE MAKING

This chapter is about the most important artistic principle in picture making: value. Nothing is more important than value when you are making two-dimensional images, especially if you are creating representational art. When you get the values correct in your images, you can do whatever you would like with the color and the picture will still work visually. If your values are wrong, no amount of color will overcome the problems associated with placing the values in the wrong place.

Value is why we can see the world around us and then interpret that world onto a 2D surface. Look at Figure 7.1. What is the picture of?

**FIGURE 7.1**    A polar bear in a blizzard.

Isn't it obvious that it's a polar bear at the North Pole during a blizzard? This figure illustrates that without the value differences, we could not see the world around us. You can prove this to yourself. Simply close the door and turn off the light in a room with no windows. Your ability to see the world around you—let alone draw that world—is dramatically crippled. Many of us have visited a cave where the guide turned out the light. You cannot see a thing because there is absolutely no value difference in the space surrounding you.

We are so dependent on value to perceive the world around us that we really do not need color at all to visually understand our environment. Black and white imagery works so well that we can often accept it as a representation of reality without any color. This is best demonstrated by the success of black and white photography.

Now that you are convinced that value is the most important principle when you are creating either traditional or digital art, let's go over a few principles that may help you use value wisely when creating your art. If you are interested in trying out the information presented here on your own, you can use just about any 2D application.

## WHAT IS VALUE?

Value is the relationship of one part or detail in an image to another part of the image with respect to either the lightness or darkness of those parts and details.

Often, we get so caught up in color we forget that without value, there would be no color. A piece of art with the correct values in the right places will be understandable even if the color is wrong. The reverse is not necessarily true. Occasionally when working on your art, convert your piece to a grayscale image. Does it still hold up visually? If you are being too influenced by color, you will quite clearly see problem areas caused by the lack of value patterns.

Most of us already know what value is. The problem comes in knowing what to do with it. The careful use of value can help you create dramatic, meaningful, and easily understood visual images. Misuse of values will lead to the viewer's visual fragmentation and confusion.

The principles of using value are the same for traditional art and computer art. In either medium, value can do three things for you, the artist, either individually or in combination: the description of objects, the expressive, and the decorative.

The most common use of value is the description of objects. We see the world around us because of the patterns and shapes created on and by objects when light falls on them. These patterns and shapes are simply the light and shadows that we see. Figure 7.2 shows a group of simple objects that are seen because of their value differences.

There are only two kinds of shadows: form shadows and cast shadows. Form shadows are the most useful for the artist because they describe the light and dark sides of objects. Everything we see has parts that either face the light or not. The transition from the light to dark can be gradual on curving surfaces or abrupt on angular surfaces. In general, the

**FIGURE 7.2**　Objects in the world are seen because of value.

more gradual the turn of a form, the softer the shadow will be. Cast shadows are pretty easy to understand. If something gets between an object and the light source, it will cast a shadow. Figure 7.3 shows both cast and form shadows.

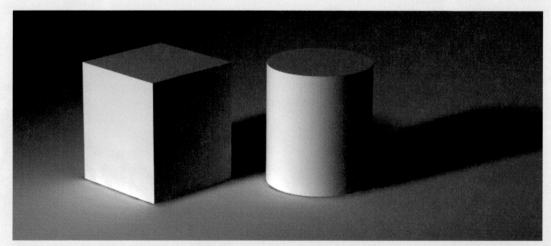

**FIGURE 7.3**　Cast and form shadows.

Each shadow gives us the visual cues we need to recognize what we are looking at. The dividing line between the light and dark sides of an object can give a good indication as to how far the object is from the light. The more shadow there is, the closer the light source is, as shown in Figure 7.4.

Likewise, the less shadow there is, the farther away the light source is, as shown in Figure 7.5.

**FIGURE 7.4**    The light source is close to the object.

Cast shadows tend to be very crisp and sharp when close to the object, gradually softening as they stretch out, as shown in Figure 7.6.

**FIGURE 7.5**    The light source is distant from the object.

**FIGURE 7.6**   A cast shadow.

The size and shape of the shadow depends on a number of conditions, including the size and distance of the light source. For this reason, cast shadows are generally not the best indicators of form, but they can be very useful in giving clues as to an object's surroundings. For example, one clue they provide is how far from another object, or background, the object casting the shadow is located. Look at Figure 7.7 and you can quite obviously tell which sphere is closer to the wall and even which sphere is larger.

**FIGURE 7.7**   Size and position in space can both be determined simply by an object's cast shadow.

Cast shadows can also give you important clues about where an object is in the environment and in relationship to the viewer. In Figure 7.8, the shadow cast by the object gives you valuable information as to where the object is in relation to the viewer, even when the object casting the shadow is out of view.

**FIGURE 7.8**    An example of the ability of a shadow to reveal important information about the object casting the shadow, even though the object is out of the field of view. You can easily surmise several things about the object, including both its position and intent.

A second use of value is the expressive. Is your work predominantly light or dark? A dark image would be appropriate if you wanted to create moody effects such as danger or sadness. On the other hand, a light image would be more appropriate for images with the opposite types of feelings. Figure 7.9 shows an example of both a predominantly light and a predominantly dark image.

A third use of value is the decorative. Using values decoratively eliminates the need for a light source in a conventional sense. This approach works best with nonrepresentational or decorative art types, as shown in Figure 7.10.

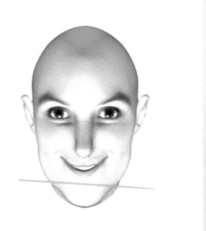

**FIGURE 7.9**    Images that are predominantly light or dark.

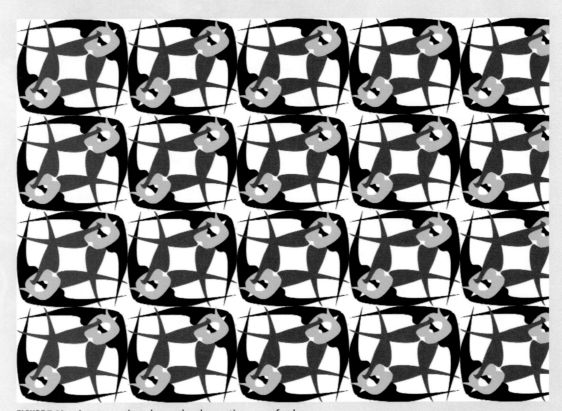

**FIGURE 7.10**    A pattern that shows the decorative use of value.

## HOW TO USE VALUE EFFECTIVELY IN YOUR ART

So, what can you do to use value to your best advantage to create easily understandable and visually dynamic art? This section suggests several ideas.

**Advancing and receding.**   First and foremost, light values generally appear to advance, and dark values appear to recede, as shown in Figure 7.11.

**FIGURE 7.11**   This image shows how values can be used to change an object's visual location within an image.

**Locating the center of interest.**   Your center of interest will always be in the light or the lightest part of a dark piece, as shown in Figure 7.12.

**Massing your values.**   Try to form an interlocking and underlying value pattern in your work to give it a sense of solidity and structure, as shown in Figure 7.13. Notice how the left side of the image looks disjointed because of the randomly placed elements. Then notice how the right half has some solidity because the elements begin to interlock and form value patterns.

**Expressing a mood.**   Have your work predominantly light or dark, depending on the mood and feeling you are trying to express. Avoid as much as possible too even a balance between the lights and darks. Figure 7.14 shows an image that is too equally balanced in value to be visually exciting.

**Getting the balance right.**   Too much balance generally leads to visually boring work. If you are having problems deciding how much dark and light value to have in your work, consider this generality. Have 60 percent of your work fall within the midrange values, have 25 percent be either light or dark, and have the remaining 15 percent be the opposite, as shown in Figure 7.15.

**FIGURE 7.12**     Keeping the lightest values and greatest contrasts in the center of interest.

**FIGURE 7.13**     Massing value as opposed to random placement.

**FIGURE 7.14**    An image whose values are too balanced.

**FIGURE 7.15**    A formula for balancing the proportions of value in an image.

**Having a full range of value within your image.**    If your piece is predominantly light, make sure that there is still an area where you have some very darks. A wide range of value will help add drama and contrast that is so needed in visually stimulating art.

**Using contrasts.**    As value contrasts increase, color contrasts decrease.

**Using intense colors.**    The most intense colors will usually be on the terminating edge between the light and dark, as shown in Figure 7.16. Here is a blue sphere being lit by a bright light. Notice that the parts of the sphere in the direct light are washed out to white, and the parts of the sphere in the shadow are black. The only area where you see the true and bright color of the sphere is on the edge between the light and dark.

**FIGURE 7.16**    A blue sphere lit by a bright light showing the color on the terminating edge between the light and shadow.

**Using gradation of light.**    As an object moves from near a light source to farther away, the light on that object will become gradually and slightly less intense, as shown in Figure 7.17.

**Drawing attention to the focal point.**    Use your greatest value changes possible at your most important center of interest. Then, gradually decrease those value changes as you move away from that focal point.

**FIGURE 7.17**    An example of a light shining on a wall. Where the light is closest to the wall, the light is most intense when compared with the light on portions of the wall that are more distant from the light.

**Using crisp changes.**    Keep your crispest changes between values at your centers of interest.

**Transitioning.**    Keep your transitions between colors of the same value soft unless you want a cutout look. In animations, the movement will do this visually.

**Using shadows.**    Warm lights need cool shadows; cool lights need warm shadows. Make sure that your shadows are consistent with the object they are associated with. For example, a light object will have a lighter shadow than a dark object's shadow.

**Using reflected lights.**    Do not let reflected lights punch visual holes into your shadows. Unless you are striving for some special effect, the reflected lights should disappear when you squint at your art.

**Using counterchange.**    Make sure that the "light" areas in your shadows are darker than the "dark" areas in your lights. A mid-value in a light area will look dark and vice versa, as shown in

**FIGURE 7.18**    Identical values may look dark in lighter areas or light in dark areas.

Figure 7.18. This is the principle of counterchange. Counterchange is a function of simultaneous contrast. Basically, counterchange is the impression that a mid-value seen simultaneously against both a light and dark ground will appear light where it is against the dark and dark where it is against the light.

## RULES FOR USING VALUE IN YOUR IMAGES

If you remember the following "rules" and apply them to your images, your work will show immediate improvement:

- Value is about relationships.
- Form is described by value.
- Nothing is more important than value in picture making.
- There are two value areas in pictures: things that face the light source (lights) and things that face away from the light source (darks).
- Mid-values are a convenient way of tying together our lights and darks and will help us create pictures that are closer to the way we see. Imagine that your mid-values are everything that is not very light or very dark. When designing your picture, try to do the basic value plan using just three values. A general guide to follow when laying out your value pattern is this: 60 percent of your values should be in the mid-value range, 25 percent should be either light or dark, and the remaining 15 percent should be the opposite. The more complicated an image is, the simpler the overall value structure should be.
- Local value is the inherent lightness or darkness of an object.
- Atmospheric value is the idea that objects of similar local value will have different atmospheric values as they recede in the picture.
- Side light value is when an object's local value will change either lighter or darker when lit from an angle.
- Simultaneous contrast causes an object's local value to appear to move toward the opposite extremes when viewed adjacent to surrounding values.
- A light image is called high key and a dark image is called low key.
- Artists tend to paint things too dark. It is easier to make the value darker than lighter. If you are not sure if the value is dark or mid-value, make it mid-value. If you are not sure what the difference between a light value and mid-value is, make it a light one.
- Work in simple values. Limit yourself to three values when you are planning out your compositions. This will help you arrange and organize your image without being caught up in unimportant detail.
- Stick to your original value plan. There is no limit to the amount of detail that you can have within a form if the form is the correct value locked into place within the composition.

- Detail is always subordinate to the overall value pattern of the composition. Detail is only incidental and descriptive.
- Keep your highest contrast between values at your center of interest.
- Value passages are important ways of unifying your pictures.
- Interlock your lights or darks.
- Use chiaroscuro to simplify your light and dark patterns. Chiaroscuro is defined as the technique of using light and shade in pictorial representation or the arrangement of light and dark elements in a pictorial work of art.
- Values on objects will gradually darken and have less contrast as they get farther away from the light source.
- Values that are in your light areas should never be as dark as the lightest areas of your darks, and vice versa.
- As value contrasts increase, color decreases. The brightest colors in your pictures may be found in the mid-values.
- The brightest colors in an object will be found in the transition edges between the lights and darks.

## CONCLUSION

There is nothing more important in making art visually understandable than value. This chapter has touched briefly on ways that you can make value work for you to make your images visually stunning and understandable. In the next chapter, we will be discussing what is probably the second most important principle in creating art: color.

# 8

# COLOR AND ITS USE IN PICTURE MAKING

Second only to value is the importance of color. Color, above and beyond all other artistic principles, is the most seductive and most expressive. We all react immediately to color. It is what we use to fire emotions in our art. Color is probably the most studied and hardest to master of all the elements of art.

This chapter quickly covers some general color concepts that you have probably heard before. This review is important because many of us could be better with our use of color. Though this chapter is not about doing exercises, you can duplicate all of these examples using virtually any piece of 2D software.

## THE FOUR PRIMARY CHARACTERISTICS OF COLOR

Color has four easily seen, understood, and measured characteristics. It is absolutely critical that all visual artists understand these characteristics.

### Hue

Hue is fairly straightforward. Hue is the base color; it is red, blue, or any other color that you can name. In light, a color can have only one hue. A light's color corresponds directly with the hue wavelength in the spectrum, as shown in Figure 8.1.

**FIGURE 8.1**   The colors of the spectrum are represented by individual hues.

The only way to change a color's hue is to mix it with another color. Mixing colors results in a completely new hue with an entirely different wavelength. Working on a computer screen is exactly the opposite of working in paint. In light, your primary colors are red, blue, and green, with your secondary colors being yellow, magenta, and cyan. Light color is an additive process where the addition of all colors will result in white light. Paint colors, on the other hand, are a subtractive process where the addition of color darkens and lessens the effect of light. Theoretically, the addition of all paint colors will result in black. Paint primaries are red, yellow, and blue, with the secondary colors being orange, green, and violet.

## Value

The value of a color is either how light or dark a color is. A color's value can be a tricky thing to understand. Some color value is easy to understand. When a blue's value is raised, and the color gets lighter, we still recognize the resulting color as blue. Red, on the other hand, is different. When we lighten the value of red, we get an entirely different color that we know as pink. The change of a color's value is shown in Figure 8.2.

**FIGURE 8.2**    A color's value is represented by how dark or light that color appears.

## Chroma

For some, the concept of chroma seems to be very hard to grasp. Chroma is simply the intensity of the hue, as shown in Figure 8.3. As a color approaches a neutral gray, it is decreasing in chroma.

**FIGURE 8.3**    Chroma is represented by how gray a color looks.

## Temperature

Color temperature (shown in Figure 8.4) is the most difficult of these four concepts to understand because it can be so relative. Usually, we think that the warm colors are yellow, orange, and red and the cool colors are green, blue, and violet. The reality is that depending on the surroundings, any color can be either warm or cool.

**FIGURE 8.4**    Temperature is represented by how warm or cool a color appears.

## SECONDARY COLOR CHARACTERISTICS

While the secondary characteristics of color are a little harder to define, they are no less important to artists as they strive for good art.

### Color Quality

Color quality is the effect of two or more colors reflected from a visually monochromatic surface. Color quality brings color to life and gives it a richness and sensuality. Take the blue squares in Figure 8.5 and compare them. The square with the subtle patterning appears much more visually exciting than the plain blue square.

**FIGURE 8.5**    Two squares of color with the same value; however, one is boring and flat, whereas the other shows good color quality.

### Color Distance

Visually, colors appear to either come forward or recede in the picture plane. This appearance is called color distance. Warm colors appear to come forward, while cool colors tend to recede. Cool colors will recede even more if their edges are soft, as shown in Figure 8.6.

### Color Weight

Color has a visual weight. Generally, the darker the color, the heavier it appears, and vice versa; the lighter the color, the lighter in weight it appears to be. A color's weight has two uses: to preserve balance and to express a visual mood. A dark color expresses strength and solidity, while a light color expresses delicacy and lightness, as shown in Figure 8.7.

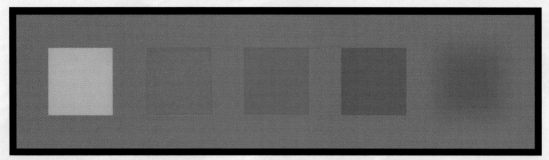

**FIGURE 8.6**    An illustration of color distance.

**FIGURE 8.7**    Color weight.

## HOW COLOR ACTS AND REACTS

This section briefly discusses how color interacts with other colors. If you know what to expect when painting, you will be able to make color work for you; you won't have to rely on happy accidents and unhappy disasters. All color is affected by surrounding color. The influence of surrounding colors brings up an interesting facet of color interaction: simultaneous contrast.

### Simultaneous Contrast

The basic theory of simultaneous contrast is that differing colors placed next to each other will enhance their differences. If you have an orange square and place it next to a red field of color, it will look more yellow.

The reverse is also true: that same orange on a field of yellow will look redder, as shown in Figure 8.8.

**FIGURE 8.8**   Simultaneous contrast between equally intense colors.

Another example of simultaneous contrast is a color surrounded by a field of gray. If the color is green, the gray will look redder; if the color is red, that same gray will look greener, as shown in Figure 8.9.

**FIGURE 8.9**   Simultaneous contrast between intense color and gray.

### Color Contrast

Color contrast is simultaneous contrast in action. Often when you are painting, the color you are using will start to do some unusual things. This is generally because of color contrast. This is especially noticeable if you are painting within a gradient, as shown in Figure 8.10. The middle rectangle is one color, but because of the gradient that it is painted into, its visual look changes dramatically.

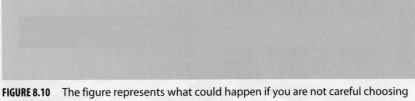

**FIGURE 8.10**    The figure represents what could happen if you are not careful choosing your colors. The middle rectangle is one color but because of the colors that it is painted in to, its visual look changes dramatically.

## USING COLORS EFFECTIVELY

Enough color theory. Here are some ideas to help you use colors more effectively when creating art:

**Do not use your colors at full strength all over your art.**    Reserve your colors of strongest intensity for your centers of interest. Color used all over at full strength will either bore or confuse your audience.

**Decide who the audience for the picture is and choose the colors accordingly.**    Be aware of gender, age, and education-level preferences.

**Different color schemes call for different handling.**    If you use a color scheme that is predominantly one color, or a family of colors, make sure that you also use a complementary color somewhere in your composition. (Near the center of interest is good.)

**If you have large fields of one flat color, break it up using "noise."**    Large expanses of flat colors are visually boring.

**Establish your color scheme quickly and stick to it.**    An established color scheme will help you keep from nitpicking individual elements and fracturing the color harmony.

**Make sure that the colors look bright.**    To make a color look brighter, place its complement next to it.

**Use a color's tendency to advance or retreat to your benefit.**    Warm color advances; cool color recedes.

**Avoid colors that are hard to read.**    Pure blue should be avoided for text, thin lines, and small shapes. Also avoid adjacent colors that differ only in the amount of blue. Avoid red and green at the edge of large images.

**A color's four main characteristics are subject to change.**    Colors change in appearance as the ambient light level changes.

**When you are changing color from one color to another it is difficult to focus on edges created by color changes alone.**

## CONCLUSION

Never forget that first and foremost, artists are doing something visual. People must be able to see what you are doing and then be able to grasp what you are saying. That is why it is so important to understand the basic principles of visual art, with value and color being the most critical. In the next chapter, we will be discussing an artistic principle that is linked closely with both value and color: lighting.

# 9

# USING LIGHTING ARRANGEMENTS TO LIGHT A CHARACTER EFFECTIVELY

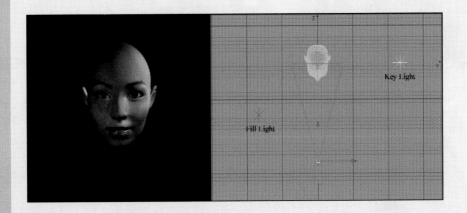

You may be wondering why a book primarily concerned with 2D painting has a chapter with examples of 3D lighting. The reason is quite simple: it is very easy to use 3D examples to describe lighting arrangements and how they work, and then explain how to apply that knowledge to 2D images. If you understand lighting, your painted and sketched images will have more strength and believability.

Some excellent and detailed books on lighting are available online or in bookstores. This chapter is not meant to supplant such valuable resources or be an all-inclusive and in-depth discussion on how to light characters or show specific positions for placing lights in 3D space. It is only a simplified overview of different lighting arrangements that are effective and have been used by traditional photographers and artists throughout the ages.

This chapter does not assume that you know a thing about 3D programs, nor is knowledge of 3D applications necessary to understand the lighting principles presented.

All of us know the importance of lighting in our images. Many times, though, artists will not give lighting much thought. Confusing and/or boring lighting schemes are usually the result.

You must remember that the casual viewer may not be the most visually astute viewer, and confusing lighting will be just as bad as boring lighting when you are trying to make your point. Good, careful lighting will help you flesh out your ideas and make them understandable. Most often, you will be using lighting as the main tool to create mood and feeling.

Look through this chapter for inspiration when you are struggling with how to light your subject or how to portray a specific mood. Look at the different lighting arrangements that are presented and you will surely find something to help you preserve and enhance the mood you are attempting to evoke when painting your character.

A basic blueprint for each lighting arrangement is given so that when you are lighting models in either 3D or real life, you will have a starting reference point to work with. Specific heights and distances from the model are not given because each individual situation requires individual attention.

## USING LIGHTING TO CREATE STRIKING ART

The most important thing when you are using lighting to create something striking—and not boring or lackluster—is to be sure of what you are trying to create. You should consider all of the following questions when planning the lighting of your character:

**What mood do you want to create?**   Do you want to create a peaceful, ominous, theatrical, or outer space effect? The mood you want will to a large degree determine where you place your lights.

**Do you want your lighting to be harsh or soft?**   A rainy day would not lend itself to any harsh direct light.

**What colors should your lights be?**   Do you want your scene to be predominantly hot or cold, or light or dark? Obviously, a dark blue light will make a darker scene. Remember that a colored light will affect all colors in a scene.

## The Main Types of Lighting

The lighting arrangements presented in the next few sections will give you ideas about lighting a scene effectively. These arrangements could be used either in 3D applications or when you're shooting reference material from living models.

### Main or Key Light

Traditionally, the most desirable light for painting or drawing has been high, north light. This light is a cool, soft light that defines form well. In our computer world, this is also a good place to start. Position your light source on a 45-degree angle from your line of sight to your target. Where you position this light source in the vertical plane should be determined by the mood that you want. It should be higher for a more natural look, and lower for a more theatrical look. This light should be the brightest. Figures 9.1 and 9.2 show two kinds of key lights.

### Secondary or Fill Light

Invariably, objects in the character's environment will reflect light into the shadows of the character. The atmosphere even does this to a certain degree. Possibly the only place where this would not happen is in deep space, where there is nothing to reflect the light back into the shadow. Yet, we have become so used to seeing this reflected light that it is represented even in space scenes. Reflected light, then, is why you will generally want a secondary light source. It's preferable to locate this light at the same vertical level or opposite angle level of the primary light, as shown in Figure 9.3.

Secondary light should be at a 50 percent or less intensity of the primary light source. It's a good idea to have your secondary light source be complementary to the primary light or neutral in color. Having a fill light

**FIGURE 9.1**    The key light is positioned high relative to the head.

that is too strong will, in most cases, begin to destroy the illusion of volume, killing form and punching visual holes into your object.

### Rim Lights

If a light source is in your field of view, you will need a rim light on your object. Placing the light at 135 degrees from your line of sight is a good starting point. You do not see a lot of rim lighting in traditional painting, but it is used extensively in contemporary illustration. Rim lights lend a sparkle to an image while helping to define form, as shown in Figure 9.4.

**FIGURE 9.2**    The key light is positioned at head level.

### Backlights

Backlights are used to separate your objects from your background. Backlights shine on the background object instead of your main object and should usually be just strong enough to separate your figure from the background. If your background light is too bright, it will tend to silhouette your figure and make it more two-dimensional. Of course, this may be just what you want. Figure 9.5 shows a very typical backlighting situation.

### Sunlight

Sunlight almost always has an equal in 3D programs. Remember that when you're trying to simulate direct sunlight in your scenes, the light

**FIGURE 9.3**    A secondary or fill light.

needs to be kept very intense. In addition, it usually casts harsh, very high-contrast, shadows. Direct sunlight can vary from white to orange depending on the time of day you are trying to represent. Indirect sunlight, such as what you see on an overcast day, can have almost any color tinge, and will generally cast very weak and soft shadows if any shadows are cast at all.

## Ambient Light

Ambient light is usually not really a light source. Rather, it is usually the amount of light bouncing around an environment that illuminates an object. Clear, sunny days may not have as much ambient illumination as foggy days. The default ambient light settings of most programs tend to be too high. As a general rule, keep the ambient light settings of all the objects

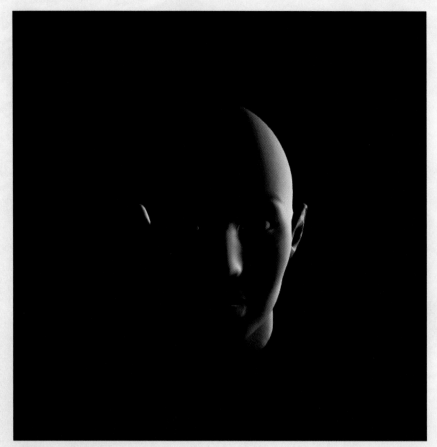

**FIGURE 9.4**    A rim light.

in your scene relatively close. If you find that the shadows in your art are just too dark and harsh, try increasing the ambient light settings.

## Positioning Your Lights

This section contains some examples of lighting setups to give you starting places for your own explorations. These examples are directly applicable to drawing and painting.

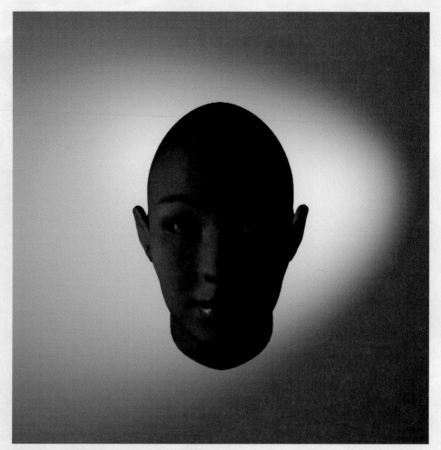

**FIGURE 9.5**    A lighting setup using backlight.

### Lighting at a 45-Degree Angle with One Light Source

Place your light at a 45-degree angle in relation to your line of sight. This lighting will produce high-contrast value patterns while doing a fairly good job of defining the target form. Almost unlimited lighting variations are available if you raise and lower the light source. Figures 9.6 and 9.7 show two examples of 45-degree lighting schemes.

### Lighting at a 45-Degree Angle with Two Light Sources

The first light is the main light source, and the second is the fill light. This scenario is identical to the previous lighting arrangement except for the addition of the fill light. If you vary the brightness of the fill along with the vertical position of both lights, the variations and control possibilities

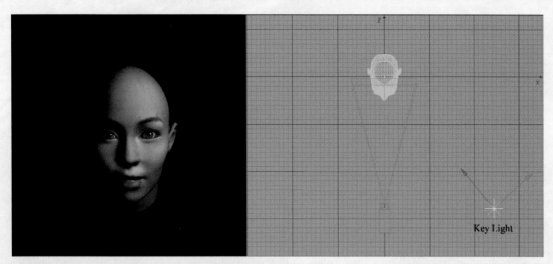

**FIGURE 9.6** An example of a very simple 45-degree lighting scheme.

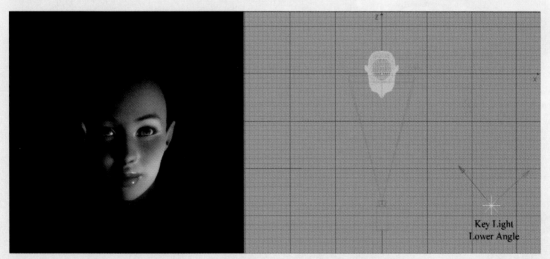

**FIGURE 9.7** Lighting at a 45-degree angle with one light source, but at a lower position.

are limitless. Figure 9.8 shows an example of a simple lighting scheme using two light sources.

### Lighting at a 90-Degree Angle with One Light Source

The light is placed at a 90-degree angle from your line of sight. The light illuminates only half of your target, with the other half remaining in total darkness. This arrangement is not nearly as useful as when you use 45-degree

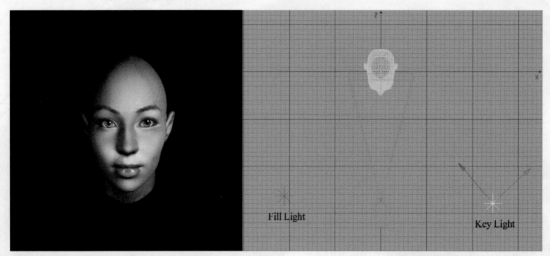

Fill Light                                    Key Light

**FIGURE 9.8** An example of lighting using two light sources.

lighting. With the 90-degree-angle scenario, form is harder to define, but you can get a nice ominous effect if that is what you are after. Again, vary the height of the light to get the feel you want. Figure 9.9 shows what happens when you are using one light source located at 90 degrees to the subject.

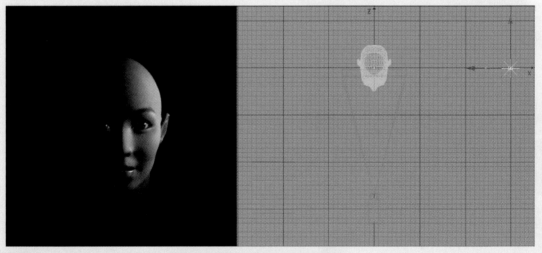

**FIGURE 9.9** Using a single light source located at 90 degrees to the subject.

In Figure 9.10, the side light is positioned at a relatively high angle to the model.

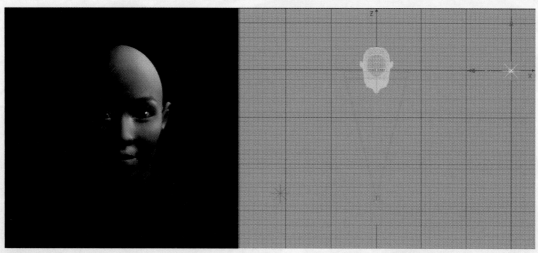

**FIGURE 9.10**    Lighting at a 90-degree angle with one light source, but at a higher angle.

### Lighting at a 90-Degree Angle with One 45-Degree-Angle Fill

The main reason for the use of the fill in this case is to lessen the abrupt transition from the darkness to the shadow. Figure 9.11 shows how a fill light will help bring out the details in the shadows.

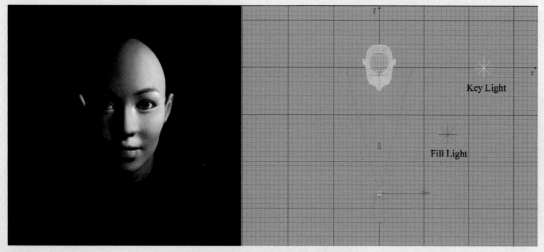

**FIGURE 9.11**    Adding one 45-degree-angle fill light to bring back detail in the shadows.

By placing the fill in the dark plane, as shown in Figure 9.12, you can add some detail back into your target. Vary the height to taste.

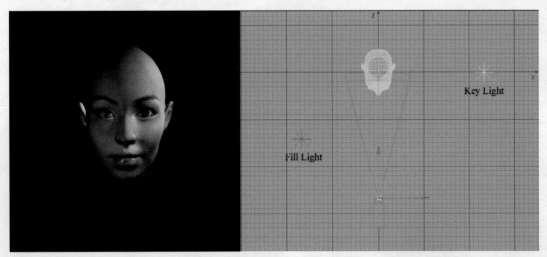

**FIGURE 9.12**   Lighting at a 90-degree angle with one 45-degree-angle fill in the dark side of the face.

### Lighting at a 135-Degree Angle

The light is placed almost behind your target. This kind of lighting is the almost ideal position for great rim lighting. Figure 9.13 shows the location of a light to produce rim lighting.

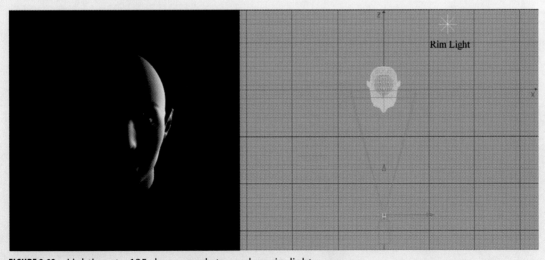

**FIGURE 9.13**   Lighting at a 135-degree angle to produce rim light.

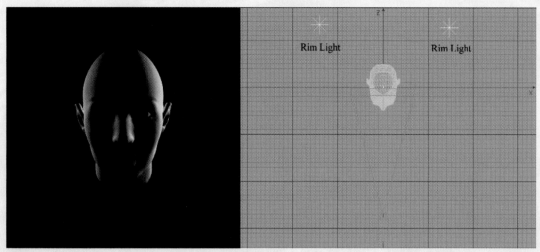

**FIGURE 9.14**    Double rim lighting.

### Front Lighting

Here, the light source is positioned very close to your line of sight. Front lighting will flatten whatever it is illuminating. Such lighting is not very useful when positioned at camera level. Figure 9.15 shows front lighting at the camera level.

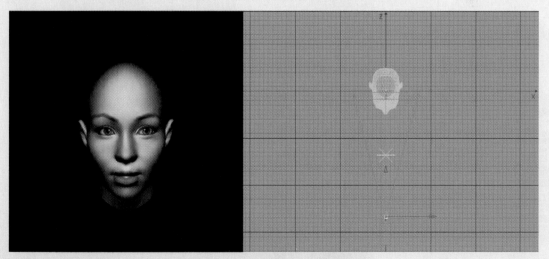

**FIGURE 9.15**    Front lighting at the camera level.

If you raise and lower the front light, good things can happen. Get the light high enough and you will get a good approximation of Rembrandt-style lighting, as shown in Figure 9.16.

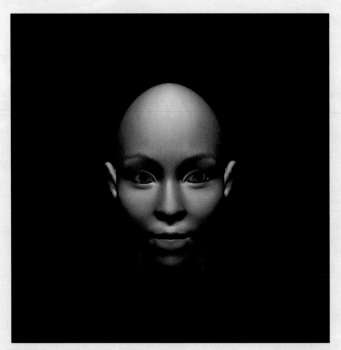

**FIGURE 9.16**    Rembrandt-style lighting.

**FIGURE 9.17**    Theatrical lighting.

If you lower the light, you will get a theatrical look that can be quite ominous if you want it to be, as shown in Figure 9.17.

## The Color of Your Lights

While it may seem obvious, you should nevertheless take great care when choosing the color of your lights. Color can enhance or destroy the effect that you are after. Figure 9.18 shows two rather unimpressive, checkered pill shapes lit by neutral white light.

Be aware of what similarly and complementary-colored lights will do to your objects. A red light will completely wash out and negate all the reds in your scene, making them appear as the whites. At the same time, a red light will make the green color appear as black, as shown in Figure 9.19.

**FIGURE 9.18**    A neutral white light.

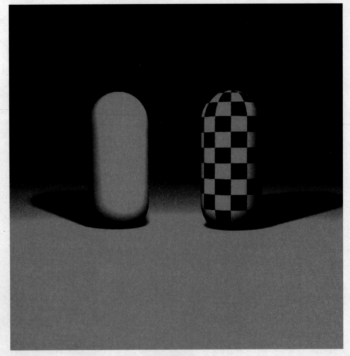

**FIGURE 9.19**    The effect of a red light.

Green lights will do exactly the opposite to your red colors, as shown in Figure 9.20.

Use colored lights where needed, especially for accent lights, but do not overuse them.

## A Last Word About Shadows

One of the beauties of 3D programs is that you can determine which objects cast and receive cast shadows. If the cast shadows do not enhance the form of the objects they are falling on, as shown in Figure 9.21, it would probably be best to eliminate their use.

The same reasoning holds true for two-dimensional works. If a cast shadow does not enhance the form that it is falling on or if it is a distraction, it is usually best to eliminate it.

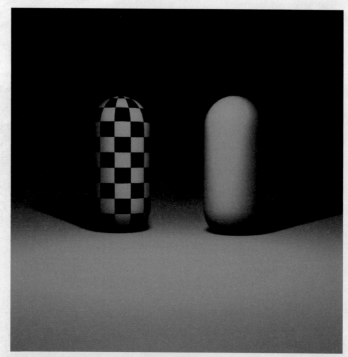

**FIGURE 9.20**    The effect of a green light.

**FIGURE 9.21**    A cast shadow that destroys the form of the object that it is cast on.

## CONCLUSION

It is hoped that this chapter gave you some different lighting ideas to consider when you are painting your character. If you are lucky enough to use a 3D program when you are designing your character, you can experiment with these variations of lighting to get just the look you are after. If you are actually going to take pictures of a living model to use as the basis for your painting, these are good starting points. As a general rule, the simplest and most straightforward lighting schemes will convey your ideas the best. Too many lights will only be confusing. In the next chapter, we will be discussing one of the most misunderstood concepts in good picture making: handling edges and edge quality.

# 10

# USING EDGES WHEN PAINTING A PICTURE

In Chapters 7 and 8, we discussed value and color as the two most important artistic principles when creating art and images. In Chapter 9, we discussed ways to use light effectively. This chapter deals with the main problem that artists have when using value and color. This problem is the edges, where differing values, colors, or both meet. You need to know how to depict the transition from one shape to the next within an image. The careful and intelligent placement of different shapes, and how you handle the edges, is at the core of successful picture making, whether decorative or representational. This chapter will discuss the different types of edges, their variations, their use, and common problems associated with edges when you are painting. While it is easy to describe the different types of edges found in art, there are no rules for their use. However, this chapter will offer some generalities that can help give you more confidence as you plan and execute your paintings, so they will become better. This chapter shows how edges interact with each other in the painting process.

## TYPES OF EDGES

You will find only five types of edges in most digital and traditional art. Not all of the different edges will always be found in each painting, but obviously there will always be at least one kind of edge present in every work of art. The five types are as follows:

**Rough/ragged edges.**    Rough edges are quite possibly the most noticeable of all the edge types and will be hard to miss when in an image. An example is shown in Figure 10.1. Depending on the technique, rough edges may be the most common type of edge within a painting. Traditionally, they are usually created using a dry-brush technique. They are much easier to create in the digital world and in just about every raster application.

**Razor-sharp edges.**    Razor-sharp edges are visually the harshest edge. An example is shown in Figure 10.2. They have a very distinct cutout appearance, as if you cut out a shape and simply laid it down on the picture plane. Traditionally, this type of edge is relatively difficult to create unless you are using some sort of masking technique. These edges are easy to create digitally and can be created by both raster and vector applications. Their use is mainly in decorative art and, in a limited way, within representational painting.

**Hard edges.**    Hard edges are just as the name suggests. An example is shown in Figure 10.3. They have a hard appearance, though not necessarily a cutout appearance. These edges will not be the most common edge found in most paintings, but they usually will be present. They are useful in attracting attention to your center of interest.

**FIGURE 10.1**   An example of a rough and/or ragged edge.

**FIGURE 10.2**   An example of a razor-sharp edge.

**Soft edges.**   Soft edges are the most common type of edge found in paintings. An example is shown in Figure 10.4. They are the most common edge because there is so much variation in their size and how they are painted. They vary in width from being almost hard to being non-edges. As with all edges, you need to know how to use them to be successful at digital painting. These edges have numerous looks. You can create them within different raster applications but you can only imitate them in vector programs.

**FIGURE 10.3**   An example of a hard edge.

**FIGURE 10.4**   An example of a soft edge.

**Non-edges or lost edges.**   The last type of edge is not really an edge at all; rather, it is more like the lack of an edge. An example is shown in Figure 10.5. As we look at the world around us, we see many instances where there are no definable edges between separate objects. This may be a function of the lighting, the amount of time that we have to look at an object, the object's distance, or any number of other reasons. If you do not see an edge, why paint an edge? This seems to be one of the hardest concepts for artists to grasp. For some reason, people seem to want to compartmentalize the world around them, and this means that individual objects have a contour. While intellectually we all know that this is true, this is not always the case visually. The lack of an edge can best be represented by an even gradation. These non-edges are some of the easiest effects to create in digital painting programs, yet their use is avoided.

**FIGURE 10.5**    An example of a non-edge.

## HOW EDGES INTERACT

When you're working with edges, you need to consider the following:

- What happens when there are numerous edges and transitions of either value or color within your painting?
- Which edges and transitions will be noticed first?
- How do you visually control which edges are noticed and which are not?

### Edges and Value

Value will most often determine which edge is visually dominant in a composition. Edges with the greatest value differences have the most visual impact, as shown in Figure 10.6. This holds true in almost all cases. A soft edge between widely different values will have more impact than a ragged edge between closer values.

**FIGURE 10.6**    Edges of greater value difference are visually more dramatic and eye catching than edges with less contrast.

Similarly painted edges will not always have the same visual impact, as you can see in Figure 10.7, where identical edges are changed only in the value contrasts between them. Those of greater contrast are visually more exciting than those of lesser contrast.

**FIGURE 10.7**    Differing visual impact between identically blended edges.

Although the edges in the example are of an identical roughness, the value between the adjacent edges is critical. Quite obviously, the more contrast there is in an edge (no matter what type of edge), the more noticeable that edge will be. While the comparison in this example is extreme, the principle nevertheless holds true.

## Edges and Color

Color hue differences will control how much visual impact there is in an edge. Intense complementary colors will give the most visually dominant edges, as shown in Figure 10.8.

**FIGURE 10.8**    Two intense complementary hues will give dramatic edges.

Unfortunately, intense complementary hued edges are dramatic as well as tiring to the eye. Hence, you should use them with great care and in small areas. Edges where one of the colors is less intense yet still complementary will still give dramatic edges but with less visual fatigue, as shown in Figure 10.9.

**FIGURE 10.9**    An edge formed by intense and muted complementary hues.

The edge formed between two neutralized hues will be the least dramatic of the complementary combinations, as shown in Figure 10.10.

**FIGURE 10.10**    Two subdued complementary hues that form an edge are not as dramatic as more intense combinations.

Analogous colored edges will be less noticeable than edges created with complementary colors, as shown in Figure 10.11. This holds true even when both edges are created with intense hues.

**FIGURE 10.11**    An edge formed by analogous colors compared to an edge formed by complementary colors.

Analogous colors that have different color temperatures will have more noticeable edges than analogous colors with similar color temperatures, as shown in Figure 10.12.

**FIGURE 10.12** Edge differences between analogous colors of different temperatures.

Color intensity will also affect how we see edges. The edge between two equally intense colors will be very dramatic and visually intense, as shown in Figure 10.13. Such an edge will be visually tiring unless used only in small areas.

The edge between an intense color and a neutral color will not be as dramatic, as shown in Figure 10.14.

**FIGURE 10.13** An edge between two equally intense and bright colors.

**FIGURE 10.14** An edge between an intense and bright color and a more neutral color.

The least dramatic edge is that based on color intensities between neutral and subdued hues, as shown in Figure 10.15.

**FIGURE 10.15**    An edge between two very neutral colors.

## WHERE YOU WILL FIND THE DIFFERENT TYPES OF EDGES

The following suggestions are intended to help you decide where you want to place different edges, where to look for edges, and how to use the different edge qualities to advantage in your work. You will use edges to lead viewers through your picture, and to get them to look at the areas you want as well as in the order that you want them to be looked at. Here are some things to keep in mind:

**Place your most interesting and visually dominant edges at the center of interest.**    The most intense and dominant edges are generally the ragged, razor sharp, and sharp ones. Place these in the following areas:

- The center of interest
- Areas that are in direct light
- The cast shadow of an object closest to the object itself
- The edges of angular objects in your picture
- An area where the local hue changes but the values remain the same, and vice versa
- Thin objects
- Wherever you want a very flat, two-dimensional effect, or a decorative effect

**You will see some edges before others.**    Use this to your advantage when planning your painting. You will see a light edge against the dark before you will see an edge made of mid-values.

You will see a hard edge before you will see a soft edge. You will see non-edges last, if at all.

**Soft edges are not noticed nearly as much as the harsher ones.**
Use this type of edge in the following places:
- Areas of your image that are not in the center of interest
- Background areas
- The shadow areas of your painting
- Areas that are lit by diffuse, soft, and indirect lights
- Cast shadows as they move away from the object that is casting the shadow
- The edges of objects that are receding in the picture plane
- Turning edges of organic forms
- Where local values change and/or local colors change
- Where you need help uniting the figure and background

**Non-edges are hardly noticeable, if perceived at all.**    Keep the following in mind:
- Non-edges are found generally in the shadow areas and areas of least interest.
- Non-edges will help keep the shadows from becoming too noticeable.
- Non-edges will provide smooth transitions for both color and value in the shadow areas.
- Non-edges can be used to provide an area of mystery.
- Most important, non-edges can help hide your mistakes.

## CONCLUSION

This is an important chapter. Edges and how you handle them in your character design will be one thing that separates your work from the ordinary. Now, we hope, you know the types of edges, where they are found, and how to use them. In Chapter 11, we will start to transition away from theory into some of the more practical aspects of painting; we will discuss blending the edges in your digital painting.

# 11

# BLENDING EDGES IN YOUR DIGITAL PAINTINGS

Blending your edges and colors in digital painting programs is not hard. Maybe it is actually too simple. In most programs, the default Airbrush tool makes it very, very easy to make gradated transitions between colors. It also makes it extremely easy to get soft edges. Some painting programs, Photoshop included, also offer a smudge or smear tool. Some talented artists use only these tools and get marvelous results. However, for the majority of digital artists, these tools leave a sterile and soulless handling of blended color and edges.

This chapter will show you two distinct things: a new method of blending color and edges using Photoshop and a method that does not really blend but gives the impression of blending.

One of the beautiful things about traditional painting is that for the most part the strokes that blend the different colors together are visible. Although this chapter is not about trying to duplicate the traditional blending of strokes, for the most part the image you are painting will be much more interesting if you can see some color variations in your blended areas.

## A NEW METHOD FOR BLENDING THE EDGE WHERE YOUR COLORS AND SHAPES MEET

This method of blending color and edges together is so simple that it really does not merit a chapter to itself, yet the technique you are going to learn is new to most digital artists. It is the method that I use for almost all blending tasks when painting in Photoshop.

The success of this method is achieved not by using any of the default Photoshop brushes or even via a combination of any of the regular tools that are used to blend. This method is based on using Photoshop's tools in new and innovative ways. It is hoped that by seeing how some common tools are used in new ways, your imagination and desire to experiment will be sparked.

Now on to blending color in Photoshop in a new and unique way. Figure 11.1 shows the image we will use as the basis for the exercise. We intentionally chose colors from all over the color wheel because such complementary colors are inherently more difficult to blend well. As you try this technique, create an image similar to this one or use the image provided on the CD-ROM.

ON THE CD

To use this method to blend colors in Photoshop, you need to do some preliminary work. The nice thing is that after you have done these few steps the first time, you will not have to repeat them the next time you use this technique.

First, create a new image of any small size. Typically, anything from $32 \times 32$ pixels square to $128 \times 128$ pixels is fine. There is no reason for it to be larger. Fill the image with any color you want, or just leave the default background color (white).

**FIGURE 11.1**    The image that will be used to blend color.

In the Edit menu, scroll down and click the Define Pattern menu item, as shown in Figure 11.2. This brings up a dialog box asking you to name your new pattern, along with a preview image of your pattern. Your preview image should look either completely white or consist of the solid color you used to fill your original image.

Go ahead and close the image you used to create your pattern. There is no need to save that image.

Now the magic begins. Pick the Healing Brush tool from the toolbar. It is the one that looks like a small adhesive bandage. Figure 11.3 shows the Healing Brush.

When the Healing Brush is selected, the options for the tool appear in the Tool Options bar at the top of the page. The size of the Healing Brush should be adjusted to suit the size of the area that you are going to blend. The larger the area, the larger the tool setting. If the brush size is particularly small, say smaller than 10, you may want to increase the size no matter how small the area you will blend. Leave the Mode setting at its default. The Source setting will default to Sampled; change this to Pattern by clicking in the small circle to the right of the word Pattern. You will now see a thumbnail appear of the currently active pattern. Click on the small down arrow next to the thumbnail and select the blank or colored pattern you created. The Healing Brush is now set to be a blending tool.

In the open image, zigzag a stroke across the borders of the colors. Do

FIGURE 11.3 The Healing Brush tool.

**FIGURE 11.2** The Define Pattern menu item.

not pay any attention to the color of the stroke. In Figure 11.4 you will notice that the stroke appears white. This is because the pattern that is being used is white. If the pattern were black or some other color, the stroke would appear either as black or as a color.

As soon as you lift the brush, the color will disappear and you will see a nicely blended stroke, as shown in Figure 11.5.

**FIGURE 11.4** The Healing Brush stroke appears to be white.

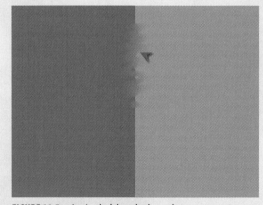

**FIGURE 11.5** A nicely blended stroke.

Quite obviously, one stroke is not going to be enough to get a good blend, so go over the area again until you get just the amount of blending that you want. Notice how much softer and controlled the blend is when multiple strokes have been used, as shown in Figure 11.6.

Experiment with different widths of strokes and brush sizes. The narrower you stroke, the smaller the blend and conversely, the larger you stroke, the larger and smoother the blend between the two colors will be. You can see the results of both small blending strokes in Figure 11.7.

**FIGURE 11.6**  Softer strokes result when you use multiple blends.

**FIGURE 11.7**  Large and small blending strokes.

There you have it: the best blending tool in Photoshop made from a tool that was not meant to be a blender.

Let's play with the shape of the brush a bit and see what happens to the blend. Figure 11.8 shows the options for the Healing Brush at the default settings. One of the first things you can change is the Hardness setting. A lower setting will give your stroke a more feathered edge. The other settings will have a more distinctive effect on the way the brush behaves. Let's change the settings to look like Figure 11.9.

Zigzag on the border between the two colors. Your stroke will look something like the one shown in Figure 11.10. The brush will be painting in a much more random manner.

When you lift your stroke, you will notice that the color is still blending but not quite as smoothly. The amount of blend will once again depend on how many strokes you overlap on each other. Figure 11.11 shows the result of the stroke using the new brush settings for the Healing Tool brush.

There is another way to vary the way the colors are blended using the Healing Brush other than changing the brush settings, and that is to change and adjust the pattern you are using. Here, subtlety is a blessing. If you have a pattern that is too distinctive, you will get something that

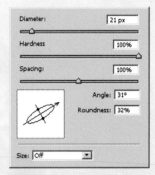

**FIGURE 11.8** The default Healing Brush.

**FIGURE 11.9** The modified Healing Brush.

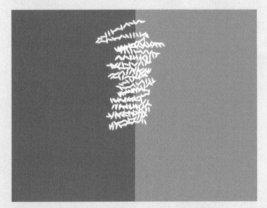

**FIGURE 11.10** The stroke using the adjusted brush.

**FIGURE 11.11** Result of the stroke using the new brush.

looks like Figure 11.12. The colors are not blending and the pattern takes over the stroke.

Let's create a pattern that will help enhance the blending of colors but not become overpowering.

Create a new image as you did earlier in the chapter. In this case, a little larger image is easier to work with than a smaller one, so make your image somewhere between 128 × 128 pixels and 256 × 256 pixels.

In the Filter menu, apply the filter Render Clouds. Figure 11.13 shows the result.

In the Image menu, select Adjustments > Brightness and Contrast, as shown in Figure 11.14.

You want to end up with an image that is so subtle in its contrast range that it is a little hard to see the differences. Save the pattern as you did earlier in the chapter. Using the Healing Brush and your new pattern, blend the colors in your image. If you have created a pattern that is subtle

FIGURE 11.12    The pattern is taking over the blending of the colors.

**FIGURE 11.13**    The Render Clouds filter applied to the image.

enough, you will have a very nice blend with a slight unevenness. Figure 11.15 shows the blended image with some unevenness in the result.

**FIGURE 11.14**    Choosing Brightness and Contrast from the menu.

**FIGURE 11.15**    The blended image created using a pattern with some noise in it.

Often this type of unevenness is preferable to a smoother blend in art. Areas that are too smooth appear boring to the eye, whereas areas with some texture will hold visual interest longer. After all, isn't holding the viewers' attention what all artists want?

You should also notice that the Healing Brush is in a menu that has more than one tool associated with the icon. Click the bandage icon and hold down your mouse button. You will notice that two other tools are available. One of them, the Color Replacement tool, is really of no use when blending with this technique, but the other one has some magic in it. The Patch tool can also be used to blend color, though in a less "painterly" way than with the Healing Brush. Choose the Patch tool and notice that Photoshop updates the toolbar with a new icon that loosely resembles a patch, as shown in Figure 11.16.

Make sure that the pattern you created is again the active pattern. Draw with the Patch tool and notice that it acts like the Lasso tool in that it creates a selection. In fact, you can hold down the Shift key to add more to the selection and the Alt key to take away from the selection. Figure 11.17 shows a selection made using the Patch tool.

**FIGURE 11.17**   A selection made using the Patch tool.

**FIGURE 11.16**   The Patch tool icon.

When you have finished making your selection, click the Use Pattern button and see what happens. As you can see, your colors are evenly blended. In fact, they are much more evenly blended than can be done by hand. The larger the selection, the larger the blend will be. Figure 11.18 shows colors blended using the Patch tool.

Another way to enhance interest when blending colors is to add a small band of color between adjacent colors. Figure 11.19 shows what I mean by this.

When you blend these colors, you will get an interesting and sometimes unpredictable result. There are two reasons for adding the band of color. One is to simply add some visual excitement to the image. The second is that sometimes when blending very complementary colors, this small band of color will make the transitions between the major colors

**FIGURE 11.18**   Colors blended using the Patch tool.

**FIGURE 11.19**    Adding a small band of color in between the two main colors.

visually smoother. Figure 11.20 shows the result of blending using a small middle band of color. Notice how the subtle greens add a visual excitement to the image.

**FIGURE 11.20**    Blending after adding a small band of color in between the two major colors.

## Optional Blending Method

Many artists use another technique to give the impression of blending colors when painting in Photoshop. This method is fundamentally different than the previous method because instead of blending the color after you have painted, you paint to give the impression that you are blending the colors.

Much of the success of this technique depends on the brush that you pick to paint with. Though most brushes work, those with anti-aliased edges will work the best. Also, brushes with the Other Dynamics box checked and an opacity jitter set to low will work very well. Figure 11.21 shows the Other Dynamics box checked and the opacity jitter set very low.

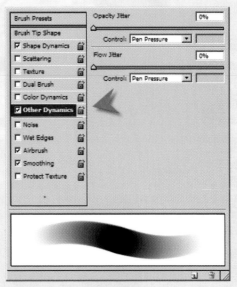

**FIGURE 11.21**   The Other Dynamics palette.

The next series of figures demonstrate how this works and just how easy the technique is to use. Follow along to better understand.

ON THE CD

Begin by creating a new image or use the original image from this chapter provided on the CD-ROM. Sample color from one side and paint into the other. Reselect color from the other side and paint back into the original side. Figure 11.22 shows colors from each side painted into the other color.

The important thing to notice is where the colors have painted over each other at less than 100% opacity. These areas are highlighted by the red arrows in the zoomed-in areas of Figure 11.22. These colors are important ones and the ones you will sample with the eyedropper to continue painting. Figure 11.23 shows an extremely zoomed-in version of the previous painting showing the intermediate colors that you will now use to paint with.

Sample some of the intermediate color and continue to paint on the edge. Notice that as the strokes are built up they become softer and softer. Continue to sample intermediate color and paint until you have nice smooth transitions between colors. Figure 11.24 shows the earlier image after additional painting on the edges using sampled intermediate colors.

This technique of painting using the intermediate colors created by individual brush strokes is the most widely used method of working in

**FIGURE 11.22**    Colors sampled from each side of the image painted into the opposite side.

**FIGURE 11.23**    A zoomed-in version of the painting clearly showing the intermediate colors created by the brush strokes.

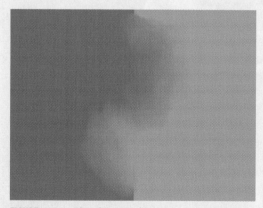

**FIGURE 11.24**    Blending can be achieved using overlapping brush strokes.

Photoshop. While this technique involves finding colors within the individual strokes and not blending existing pixels, it is an important method of painting within Photoshop. We included it in this chapter because the results are similar and meant to emulate the blending of colors.

## CONCLUSION

You can now see how easy it is to blend colors in Photoshop. Using these simple techniques will give your paintings a life that far exceeds the look that is possible using only the Airbrush or Smudge tool. In the next chapter, we will explore ways to use textures in your Photoshop paintings.

# 12

# CREATING TEXTURES AND PATTERNS FOR USE IN DIGITAL PAINTING

When you're learning to paint on the computer, one of the most important skills you can master is being able to create and paint with texture. If you paint with texture, you can produce effects that would be tedious, if not impossible, to do with traditional methods. Not only are you able to create such effects but you can do so quickly.

This chapter will show you how to go about creating custom textures from photographs, by using Photoshop's Pattern Maker and by hand-drawing patterns. While these methods are demonstrated in Photoshop, most of the techniques shown are applicable with other painting applications.

Just so there is no confusion, within Photoshop, textures are called patterns. The terms are interchangeable for our purposes.

*ON THE CD*

In the Chapter 12 folder on the CD-ROM, you'll find a group of textures selected and created especially for this chapter.

## CREATING TEXTURES

As when creating textures for 3D applications, you need to remember a few things when creating textures for use in 2D paint programs:

**The size of the texture is important.** 2D paint programs hold the texture in memory when you are using them to paint. Having somewhat smaller textures will increase the speed at which you can work. You can have and use large textures, and artists often do for specific projects. However, typically textures should be rather small, usually less than 512 × 512 pixels in dimension. More often than not, it's best to try to keep your textures 256 × 256 pixels in dimension.

**Contrast is important.** Most paint programs use the value information in an image to create the texture. Having images with narrow value ranges will not provide as effective textures as will images with a large range of values. The opposite can also be true. A strictly black and white image will often prove to be too contrasty and harsh.

**Seamless is generally better.** It's not very desirable to be in the middle of painting and suddenly have a line appear in your image where the texture ends. Try to always make the textures that you use seamless so that their edges will not become a distraction.

There are three main methods of creating textures in the digital world: taking and manipulating images from the real world; using computer applications, in this case Photoshop, that are capable of creating textures; and drawing your own by hand.

## Creating Textures from Photographic Reference Materials

The main requirement for creating textures from photo reference is to be aware of your surroundings. If you cannot see the textural surfaces around you, you will not be able to use them. You might want to get in the habit of carrying a camera around with you. You never know when something will catch your eye and will be usable in an image you are contemplating.

You can use a digital camera to photograph the textures that you see around you. Film cameras as well as scanners are also useful. Whatever you use to get the image is really not important, as long as you get the image. An inexpensive digital camera with a two-megapixel image will serve you just as well as an expensive, higher-resolution one. Digital is preferable because it is so easy to get the image into the computer. Figures 12.1 through 12.3 are digital pictures of some natural textures found in Goblin Valley State Park.

**FIGURE 12.1**   Texture number 1.

**FIGURE 12.2**   Texture number 2.

**FIGURE 12.3**   Texture number 3.

These images are good beginnings for drawing some great textures in your paintings, but they're not really usable in their current form. To get the images ready to be used as textures within Photoshop, follow these steps:

1. Pick any of the three images and resize it from 2048 × 1536 pixels to 400 × 300.
2. In the Filter menu, select Other and then Offset. In the resulting dialog box, offset the image 200 pixels in the horizontal direction and 150 pixels in the vertical direction. Make sure the circle next to Wrap Around is checked. Your image will now look like the one in Figure 12.4. Now it is quite obvious where the seams of the image are located. With the sides of the image moved into the center, it is time to get rid of the seams and have a texture that can be tiled.

**FIGURE 12.4**    The texture with offset applied.

3. There are several methods you can use to get rid of these seams in Photoshop. Each has different strengths and weaknesses. You can use the Clone Stamp tool, the Healing Brush tool, and the feathered cut-and-paste technique. Usually a combination of all three will bring you the best results.

   To use the cut-and-paste method, do the following. Using the rectangular selection tool, select a relatively thin selection of the image that is almost the whole vertical height of the image, as shown in Figure 12.5.

   Feather the selection about 5 pixels, then copy and paste the selection. You can see the part that is copied and pasted in Figure 12.6.

**FIGURE 12.5**    The tall, vertical selection.

**FIGURE 12.6**    The selection that is cut and pasted.

Place this feathered selection over the middle seam of your image. Move it up or down to get a good random placement. Often you may need to paste several pieces to get good coverage of the vertical seam. When you have covered the vertical seam to your liking, merge down all the layers.

4. Now do the same thing in the horizontal direction. Make a long horizontal selection, feather the selection, copy it, and paste it back into the image. Figure 12.7 shows the horizontal selection that will be pasted back into the image.

Once again, it might take more than one paste operation to cover the horizontal seam completely. Figure 12.8 shows the texture with all the seams now covered.

**FIGURE 12.7**    The feathered horizontal selection.

**FIGURE 12.8**    The texture with both the horizontal and vertical seams covered.

When the seams are covered to your satisfaction, go ahead and merge all the layers down.

5. Increase the contrast of the image, as shown in Figure 12.9. You can do this in Image >Adjustments >Brightness and Contrast or Image >Adjustments >Auto Contrast.

**FIGURE 12.9**    The texture with the contrast increased.

6. You will notice that there is still some unevenness in the image along the horizontal and vertical areas where the original seams were. This value difference needs to be minimized as much as possible or your image will appear distinctly repetitive when used as a pattern. There

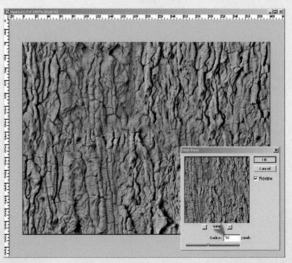

**FIGURE 12.10**    The texture with the High Pass dialog box displayed.

is a simple way to minimize these large value differences by using the High Pass filter (from the Filter menu, choose Other and then choose High Pass). Figure 12.10 shows the High Pass filter slider with a radius setting of 10 pixels and the resulting change in the image. Play with the slider until you remove as much of the value shift across the image as possible. The High Pass filter is extremely good at removing the low-frequency noise from images. You will notice that it also removes most of the color, but this is not really a concern when creating textures to paint with.

7. Run the Auto Levels adjustment to get a good range of values from dark to light. Figure 12.11 shows the texture after adjusting the levels.

8. Let's now save the newly created seamless texture as a pattern and have it available to use in your paintings. This is as simple as going to the Edit menu and selecting Define Pattern. Figure 12.12 shows the location of this command. Choosing it will bring up a dialog box asking what you want to call your new pattern. Call it whatever you like, but make it something you can remember. After defining your pattern, it is a good idea to go ahead and save the image you have

**FIGURE 12.11**    The texture after running the Auto Levels command.

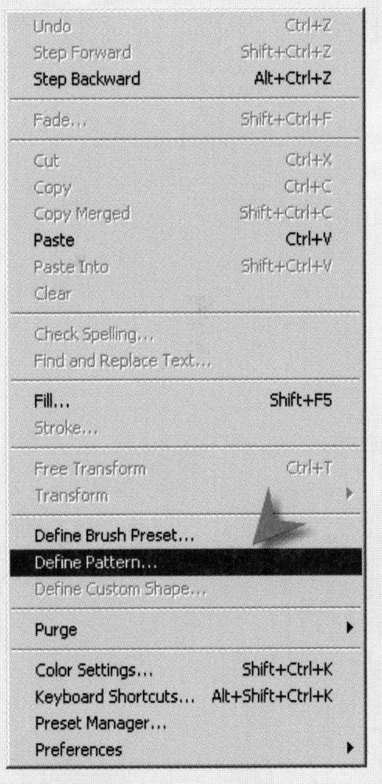

**FIGURE 12.12**    The Define Pattern command found under the Edit menu.

been working with. You never know when you might need this image again.

Just as with brushes, when you have created a few of your own new and unique patterns, save them into your own pattern libraries.

### Photoshop's Pattern Maker

Both Photoshop 7 and CS have a nifty little item nestled under the Filter menu called Pattern Maker. Pattern Maker has the potential of generating a virtually endless supply of seamless patterns. It uses information from either a selection within an image or the contents of the Clipboard. You can create multiple patterns from a single selection.

In this section, we will quickly go over creating various textures using Photoshop's Pattern Maker from a photographic reference.

First, open any of the photographs of textures supplied on the CD-ROM and select the Pattern Maker from the Filter menu, as shown in Figure 12.13.

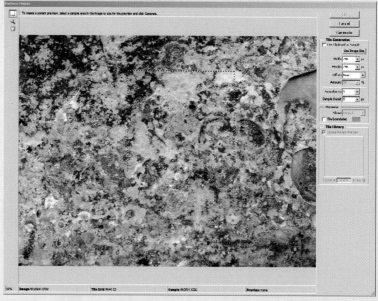

**FIGURE 12.13**    The Pattern Maker.

You will notice that your cursor has turned into a crosshair. Use this to select a region with the image. You can move the selection around by clicking and holding within the selection.

After selecting the area you want to use to make the pattern, you need to tell Photoshop what size you want the seamless tile to be. These controls are found in the Tile Generation section of the Pattern Maker. You can have the tile be the whole image size, which will make the tiling image the same size as the original image. You can also enter numeric values in the width and height fields, or drag the sliders that will pop up when you click on the small triangle to the right of the numbers.

If you want the tile to offset in either the vertical or horizontal direction, select Vertical or Horizontal in the Offset box. The default is No Offset. Below the Offset box is the amount of offset. This is a percentage of the pixel dimensions you specified.

Now, click the Generate button at the top of the Pattern Maker window. The preview area where the original texture or photo was displayed is now filled with the created pattern/texture, as shown in Figure 12.14.

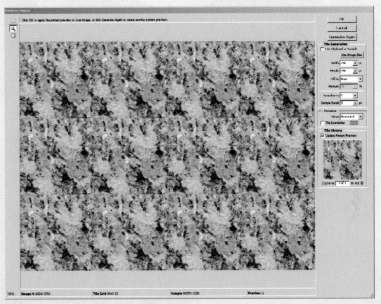

**FIGURE 12.14**   The Pattern Maker window is filled with the generated pattern/texture.

The individual tile is displayed in the preview window in the Tile History section of the Pattern Maker. You can also preview the tile boundaries and how the individual tiles line up within the larger image by checking the Tile Boundaries box.

If you like the texture that is created, click on the small floppy icon right below the preview window. This will bring up the Pattern Name dialog box, shown in Figure 12.15.

Name the pattern, and Photoshop then saves it into your current library. You can quickly generate an extremely large number of variations

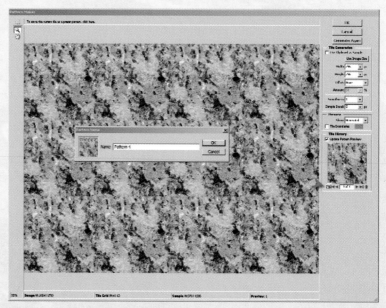

**FIGURE 12.15**   The Pattern Name dialog box appears when you click on the small floppy logo below the preview window.

if you want by clicking the Generate Again button. As each pattern is generated, the preview will update. After a few (or many) patterns are generated, you can cycle through them using the arrows below the preview window. Save the ones you like and discard the ones you don't by clicking on the small trash can icon. You can generate up to 20 tiles before the Pattern Maker begins to delete the oldest in the series.

Now you have seen two ways of creating seamless textures to use in your Photoshop painting projects. There is one more method worth mentioning, and that is creating your textures by hand. While not the fastest method by any measure, it is the method where you have the most control over what you create. In the next section, you will see the general method used to create a texture by hand.

### Creating Hand-Drawn Textures from Scratch

This may become your favorite method for creating textures. The method is relatively straightforward and easy to master. The variety of textures possible is limited only by your imagination. Follow these steps to draw textures by hand using Photoshop:

1. Create a new image of any size up to about 600 × 600 pixels. Select any brush that you care to use and begin drawing and painting in the center of the image, as shown in Figure 12.16.

2. In the Filter menu, select Other and then choose Offset. Make sure Wrap Around is selected and offset the image half its dimensions in both the vertical and horizontal directions. The image will have something of a cross shape in the middle, as shown in Figure 12.17.

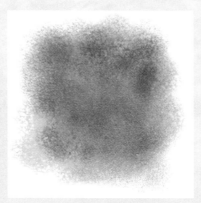

**FIGURE 12.16**    Begin painting in the texture, at first limiting your work to the center of the image.

**FIGURE 12.17**    The texture offset in both the horizontal and vertical directions.

3. Continue to paint in the center of the image, working toward the edges but not touching them, as shown in Figure 12.18.
4. Once again, offset the image but only one quarter of the dimensions this time. You now have only a couple of white areas located in opposite corners. Fill in these areas using your same brushes, as shown in Figure 12.19.

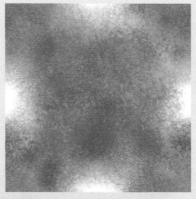

**FIGURE 12.18**    Using the same brushes and painting in the center of the image.

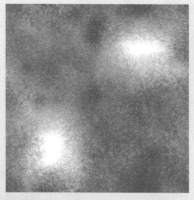

**FIGURE 12.19**    The image offset again but only one quarter of the dimensions.

5. As Figure 12.20 shows, you now have a completely seamless texture that you can convert into a pattern and use in your painting.

**FIGURE 12.20**   The completely hand-drawn custom texture.

## CONCLUSION

This chapter has shown you three ways to create textures for use in digital paintings. There are, of course, as many ways of making textures as there are of creating digital art. The techniques shown here should be only a jumping point for your own explorations. In the next chapter, we will go over Photoshop's powerful brushes. You will learn how to manipulate the default brushes to get them to behave as you would like, and you will learn how to create your own completely new, custom brushes.

# 13

# PHOTOSHOP BRUSHES

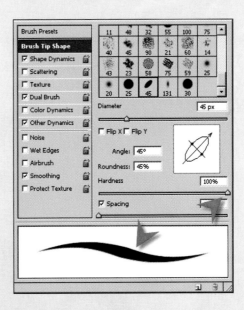

## Section 1: The Basics of Photoshop Brushes

Many, many books have been published on how to use Photoshop. Because so many good materials are already available, we are not going to delve into all of the deep nooks and crannies of the program. This is a book on digital painting, and we will concentrate on what is most important to our task at hand: brushes and how to make them do what you want.

In this chapter, you will learn and/or refresh your memory on a number of different ways to access and use Photoshop's brushes. You will learn how to make a brush behave like you want. We will go over each of the palette and menu options that Photoshop gives you to control the look and feel of individual brushes. This will be a rather lengthy chapter, as we will look at each of the options available. Have patience; if you learn how to control Photoshop's brushes now, your productivity and creativity will be increased dramatically as you create your paintings.

Remember that for the most part you may want to use only one or two brushes for any given painting. Sometimes you will use a few more brushes but almost never will you want to use everything that is at your disposal. To be able to make those decisions you need to know

- Where Photoshop's brushes are located and how to access them
- How to change the basic properties of a brush
- The brush options available to you in the Brushes palette

## Where Are the Photoshop Brushes?

While this may seem obvious, there may be a few of you who don't know where the brushes are located. Never fear; they are easy to find. Figure 13.1 shows the location of the Brush tool in Photoshop.

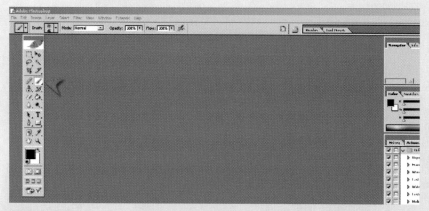

**FIGURE 13.1**    The location of the Brush tool in Photoshop.

The Brush tool is the fourth icon on the left side of the toolbar. If you click this icon and hold down your mouse button, the icon will change to the Pencil tool. Figure 13.2 shows the Pencil tool.

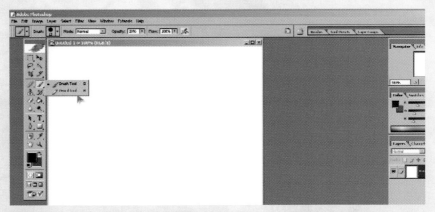

**FIGURE 13.2**    The submenu item showing the Brush tool and the Pencil tool.

The Pencil tool is a very small version of the brush. You can increase its size, but you should have no reason to do so. Leave the Pencil tool small for fine work and use the Brush tool for painting. The keyboard shortcut is "B" for both tools.

When you click the Brush icon, notice that the Options bar at the top of the screen changes to reflect the currently selected tool, as shown in Figure 13.3.

The first icon on the Options bar is the Tool Preset Picker. When the Brush tool is selected and the Preset Picker activated, Photoshop displays three brushes by default. This is a great place to add and store your most

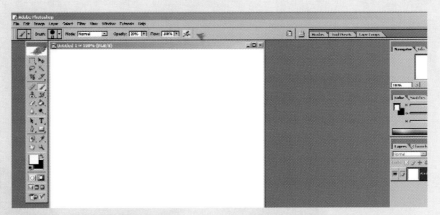

**FIGURE 13.3**    The Brush Options bar.

commonly used brushes to have them close for easy access. Figure 13.4 shows the Tool Preset Picker menu.

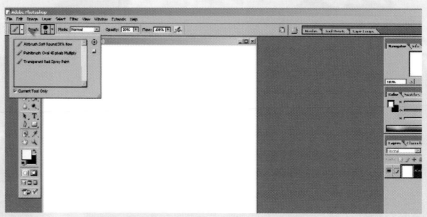

**FIGURE 13.4**    The Tool Preset Picker menu.

New in Photoshop CS is also a Tool Presets tab (Figure 13.5) that also stores your most commonly used brushes along with any other frequently used tools you may care to add. It is located on the right side of the Photoshop screen next to the Brushes tab.

**FIGURE 13.5**    The Tool Presets tab.

The next icon on the Options bar is the Brush Picker (Figure 13.6). Click this icon and you will be presented with a visual display of all your currently loaded brushes. The default selection is large and presents you with more than enough brushes to paint almost anything with. You will

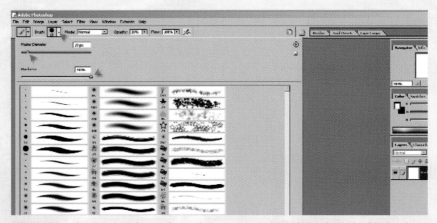

**FIGURE 13.6**   The Brush Picker with Brush Diameter and Brush Hardness highlighted.

also notice two controls that are available when this palette is open: Brush Diameter and Brush Hardness (indicated by red arrows).

You have a number of options for previewing what your brush looks like. The default display, shown in Figure 13.6, shows a small icon of the brush profile and what a typical stroke will look like. Sometimes you may want to switch to a larger display of the brush profile. You access the control panel for the Brush Picker by clicking on the small triangle within the circle on the right side of the picker. Clicking on the triangle will give you a number of options for displaying your brushes along with available brush libraries you can load. Figure 13.7 shows the Brush Picker with the large thumbnail option selected within the control panel.

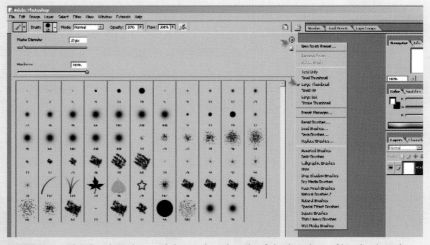

**FIGURE 13.7**   The Brush Picker with large thumbnails of the brush profiles displayed.

The third item on the Options bar is the mode selector (Figure 13.8). These modes are similar to the modes that you can apply to individual layers. You must remember, though, that unlike layers that can be deleted, changed, and manipulated, brush modes are permanent in comparison. Notice also that Behind and Clear are grayed out in the menu. This is because these modes do not work on the background layer. Refer to the Photoshop manual for a more in-depth discussion of the modes.

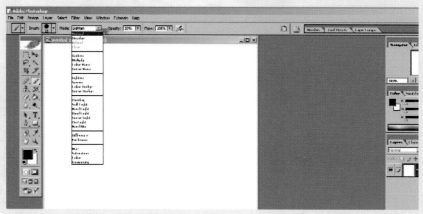

**FIGURE 13.8**  The Brush Mode menu.

The next menu item on the Options bar is Opacity. This option is self-explanatory; it lets you specify how opaque or transparent individual pixels will appear when you are painting. Figure 13.9 shows the same brush using various opacities for its strokes.

**FIGURE 13.9**  The Brush Opacity slider along with an image showing strokes using various opacity settings.

When you decrease the opacity of the stroke, you are able to see the underlying strokes. You can alter the opacity of the stroke by using the slider under the Opacity setting or by entering a numerical value.

The next-to-last item on the Options bar is Flow. Flow visually looks fairly similar to Opacity but isn't. The Flow slider determines how quickly and evenly your digital paint is applied. When you use a high setting, the pixels are filled in quickly and very closely spaced together. As you gradually reduce the flow, the pixels are not filled in as quickly or as evenly. You can see the results of gradually reducing the flow in Figure 13.10. As with the opacity, you can change the amount of flow by moving the slider or entering a value.

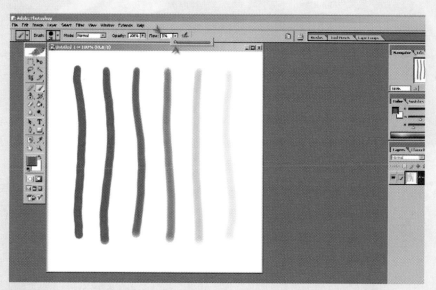

**FIGURE 13.10**   The Flow slider and an image showing strokes using different flow settings.

The final item on the Options bar is the Airbrush icon, shown in Figure 13.11. Clicking and holding this icon will cause digital paint to be deposited as long as you hold your stylus pressed to the tablet. It will do the same if you are painting with the mouse and hold down the left mouse button.

Moving across the Options bar you are able to pick a brush preset. Using that preset you can paint in any of a number of different modes selected from the drop-down list. Once you have selected the brush profile and mode, you can then change either the brush opacity or brush flow, or both. Finally, by clicking the Airbrush icon, you can determine if the brush will continuously deposit paint while holding down either the left mouse button or your stylus.

It is also worth noting that you can change the default size and opacity of your brushes using keyboard shortcuts. Using keyboard shortcuts

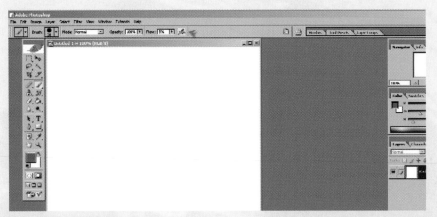

**FIGURE 13.11**    The Airbrush icon.

can dramatically increase your speed when painting. Consult your Photoshop documentation for the specific shortcut keys for the brushes.

That's about it for our simple explanation of how to pick a brush and change a few of the brush settings using the Options bar.

In the next section, we will dig deeper into the workings of the more advanced brush controls available in Photoshop.

## SECTION 2: THE PHOTOSHOP BRUSHES PALETTE

While the Options bar gives you some control over how your brush will behave, the Brushes palette is where the fun really begins. Using this palette, you can control virtually any aspect of how your brush acts.

The Brushes palette is one of the tabs located just to the right of the Brush Options bar (Figure 13.12). Click on the tab and let's look at what is revealed. This palette will stay visible until you click somewhere on the screen.

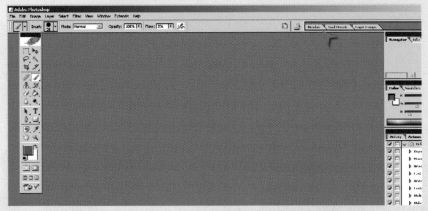

**FIGURE 13.12**    The Brush tab.

You can also quickly access the options for your currently active brush by clicking the Toggle the Brushes Palette icon located on the far right of the Options bar, as shown in Figure 13.13.

**FIGURE 13.13**    The Brushes Toggle icon.

The Brushes palette can look daunting when opened, as you can see in Figure 13.14. So many controls are available that it can be overwhelming deciding where to start. Should you begin with the Shape Dynamic controls? Or the Scattering controls? Texture? Dual Brush? Color Dynamics? There are just too many options!

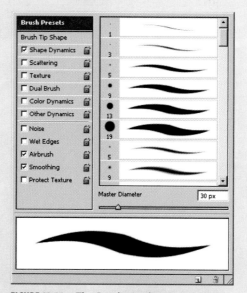

**FIGURE 13.14**    The Brushes palette.

To make things as simple as possible, let's start at the top and work our way down the palette settings. The first thing to notice is the far-left edge of the palette. Here you will see a number of small boxes. These boxes will either be checked or not checked, depending on the brush that you currently have selected. A check means that the option is currently active for the brush you are using. Clicking on the small padlock icon locks those options for the current brush. These boxes and icons are highlighted with red arrows in Figure 13.15.

The first two options are different in that they do not have a small check box to their left. This may cause you to overlook these first and very basic controls, the Brush Presets and the Brush Tip Shape.

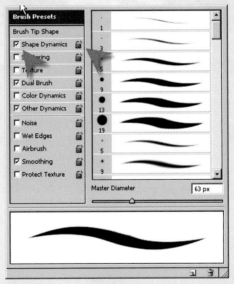

**FIGURE 13.15**     The option boxes and padlock icons located in the Brushes palette.

## Brush Presets

The Brush Presets are self-explanatory; they simply display the brushes that are currently loaded within Photoshop, as shown in Figure 13.16.

## Brush Tip Shape

Click on the Brush Tip Shape option and you get the palette shown in Figure 13.17.

In this first palette you set some of the very basic parameters of the brush you will be creating or using. This palette displays the brush tips that Photoshop currently has loaded. Within the default brushes, you will

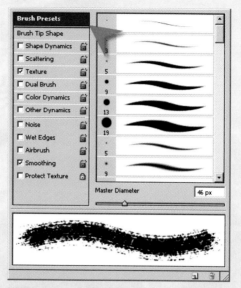

**FIGURE 13.16**    The Brush Presets located in the Brushes palette.

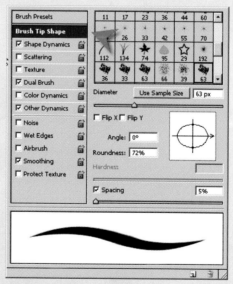

**FIGURE 13.17**    The Brush Tip Shape menu located in the Brushes palette.

notice brushes ranging from simple round brushes to leaf shapes. Also displayed at the bottom of the palette is a preview of your currently selected brush that reflects the current brush settings. You can change brush tips by clicking any of the small icons showing the brush profile. If you are simply going to change the brush you are currently using, do not click any of these different brush tips.

To show how some of the other controls function within this palette, select the hard elliptical 45 brush, as shown in Figure 13.18.

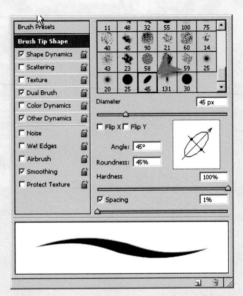

**FIGURE 13.18** Selecting the hard elliptical 45 brush.

Right under the brush tip display you notice the first control: the Diameter slider. You will also see a box showing the current diameter of the brush tip. You can move this slider up or down to change the diameter of the brush tip and display an update of what the brush will look like in the preview window at the bottom of the palette. You can also click your cursor in the box and enter a numerical value for the diameter if you wish. Below are two small boxes called *flip x* and *flip y*. Checking one of these boxes will flip the brush on either its x- or y-axis; if you check both, Photoshop will flip the brush on both axes. The larger display to the right (showing an ellipse with an arrow aligned along its major axis and two dots aligned on the shorter axis) contains the Angle and Roundness controls. There are also two boxes labeled Angle and Roundness; they display the current angle that the brush is aligned to and how round the brush is. In our current brush, the angle alignment is 45° to the right with a roundness of 45% of a circle. You can change these values either by entering numeric values in the boxes or by using the displayed ellipse. To change the angle, click and drag on the major axis displayed as the arrow. To change the roundness, click and drag on one of the two dots on the minor axis. Figure 13.19 shows the Angle and Roundness controls.

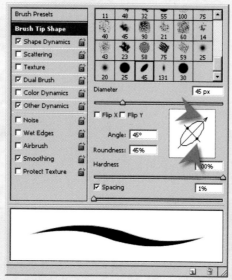

**FIGURE 13.19**    The Angle and Roundness controls.

The next slider below the Angle and Roundness controls is the Hardness slider with a range from 0% to 100%. At the 100% setting, you see that the edges of the brush displayed in the preview are very crisp (Figure 13.20). If you drag the slider down to the left or enter a different numeric value, you will see how the edge grows progressively softer in the brush preview window (Figure 13.21).

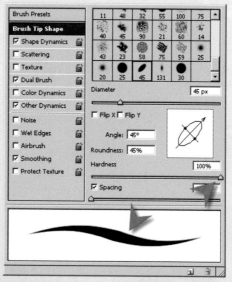

**FIGURE 13.20**    The Hardness slider and brush preview window.

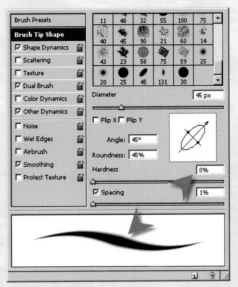

**FIGURE 13.21**     Moving the Hardness slider
down gives a softer stroke.

The final control in this portion of the brush settings palette is the Spacing control. This consists of a slider and a check box, and determines how closely together Photoshop will put the individual brush dabs. Currently, the check box is selected and the preview window shows your brush stroke with very smooth and close spacing, as shown in Figure 13.22.

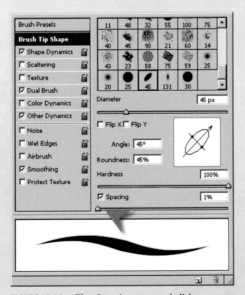

**FIGURE 13.22**     The Spacing control slider.

Now notice what happens when you move the Spacing slider up to a higher value. You begin to see more and more space between the brush dabs until you can actually see the individual dabs, as shown in Figure 13.23.

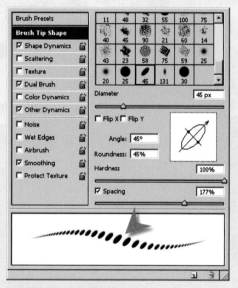

**FIGURE 13.23**    Moving the slider up on the Spacing control puts increasing amounts of space between paint dabs.

Unchecking the Spacing box takes away the control you have over the dab spacing and will give you a random result (Figure 13.24) unless you have a steady hand. The stroke where the dabs appear closer together is made by moving the stylus very slowly; moving the stylus quickly results in more space between the dabs.

## Shape Dynamics

The next option is called Shape Dynamics. Click on this menu item to open the palette shown in Figure 13.25. Deselect the Shape Dynamics box and notice what happens to your stroke within the preview window (Figure 13.26). Along with showing a stroke that now has very little size variation within it, Photoshop grays out all of the menu options.

Now check the Shape Dynamics box to activate the Shape Dynamics palette. Within this palette you will find six controls. The first slider at the top of the palette is Size Jitter, with a box immediately below giving you a menu that lets you control the effect. Move the small arrow to the right

**FIGURE 13.24** Random spacing in the brush stroke caused by deselecting the Spacing box.

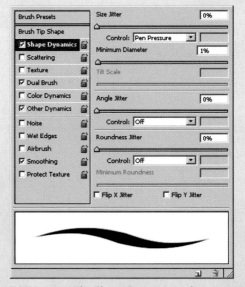

**FIGURE 13.25** The Shape Dynamics palette.

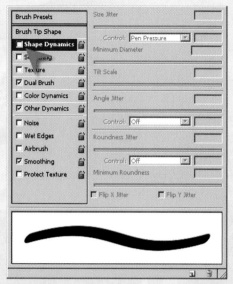

**FIGURE 13.26**    Deselecting the Shape Dynamics options and the results.

and notice what happens within the preview window. The size of the individual brush dabs begins to vary and the stroke looks rougher and more random, as shown in Figure 13.27.

The next control is the Minimum Diameter slider, shown in Figure 13.28. This slider set to a low value will make the brush dabs very small

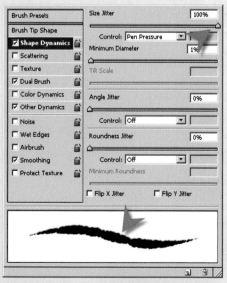

**FIGURE 13.27**    Moving the Size Jitter slider to the right gives a more random stroke.

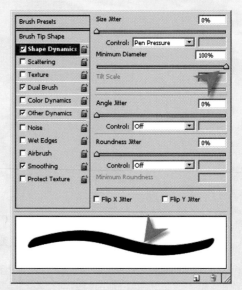

**FIGURE 13.28**    The Minimum Diameter slider.

at the beginning of a stroke. Move the slider up, and the beginning dabs will get progressively larger. At the maximum setting, there will be no variation of size within the stroke.

Angle Jitter is the next control. Most of these controls are self-explanatory, and this one is no exception. With the Angle Jitter set to 0%, as shown in Figure 13.29, the angles of the brush dabs remain for the most part identical.

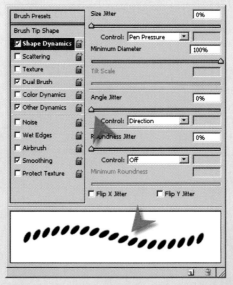

**FIGURE 13.29**    The Angle Jitter set to 0%.

Move the slider up or enter a numeric value, and the angle of the brush dabs begins to vary, as shown in Figure 13.30. The brush dab spacing has been increased to show the effect more clearly. Once again you can pick the control method for the effect.

The next control is Roundness Jitter, shown in Figure 13.31. This control will vary the roundness of the brush dabs as you paint. As you raise the value by typing in a value or moving the slider, you can see the

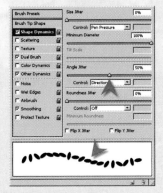

**FIGURE 13.30**    Increasing the Angle Jitter slider.

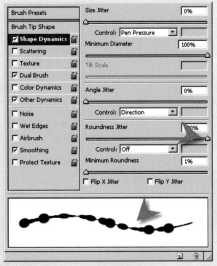

**FIGURE 13.31**    The Roundness Jitter slider.

results in the preview window. The roundness of the dabs vary from very thin to round. You can use the Roundness Jitter control in conjunction with the Minimum Roundness slider. Setting the slider low will make the dabs very thin and higher values will make the dabs rounder.

## Scattering

Check the Scattering box to activate the Scattering palette, shown in Figure 13.32. This control does exactly what it says: it scatters the brush dabs within the brush stroke. The more the slider is moved to the right, the more the individual dabs will be offset from the stroke of the stylus. Check the Both Axes box and the dabs will be scattered in a more random fashion along both axes. Eventually, if the scatter is set high enough, the direction of the original stroke can virtually disappear, as Figure 13.33 shows.

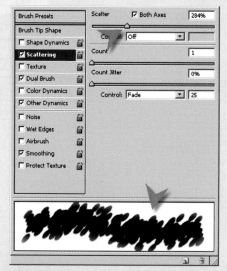

**FIGURE 13.32**    The Scattering palette lets you "scatter" the brush dabs.

Below the Scatter slider are two additional sliders. The first is Count, and it does just what the name implies. From the lowest value of 1 to the maximum value of 100, as you move the slider to the right you increase the number of dabs that will be scattered. Below the Count slider is the Count Jitter slider, with a control box below the slider (Figure 13.34). The control box sets what drives the effect. To see the results most clearly, set the control to Fade and move the Count Jitter slider all the way to the right. You will notice that a higher amount of jittery dabs begin at the start of the stroke and "fade" as the stroke moves to the right. Experiment with additional settings to see the result.

**FIGURE 13.33**    A stroke with a very high Scatter setting.

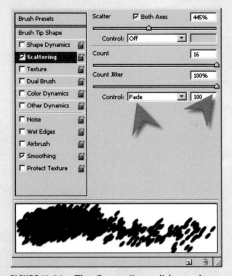

**FIGURE 13.34**    The Count Jitter slider and menu for picking what will drive the effect.

## Texture

The next series of controls are in the Texture palette (Figure 13.35). Checking the Texture box will mix the currently selected pattern with your brush stroke. You can select a different pattern within the Texture palette by clicking the patterns thumbnail. You can also invert the pattern and see how it reacts by checking the small box just to the right of the pattern thumbnail.

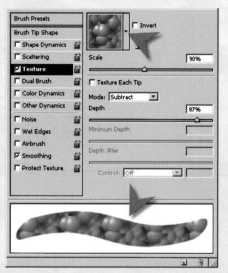

**FIGURE 13.35**   The Texture palette showing a selected pattern and its effect on the brush stroke.

Below the preview image is a slider that you can use to vary the scale of the selected pattern. You will also notice the mode selector, where you can select how the pattern will interact with the brush stroke. These modes are similar to the layer modes you are familiar with. The Depth slider determines how much of the pattern will interact with the stroke. A low value means that very little of the pattern will interact, while a higher value means that more of the pattern will be visible within your stroke. You can also enter a numeric value in the box above the slider. The two remaining sliders are available only if you have the Texture Each Tip box checked right above the mode selector. Figure 13.36 shows the results of adding Depth and Depth Jitter to a brush.

These controls obviously work best if you have a brush with multiple tips. Experiment with the sliders at different settings to get a variety of nice, rough brush strokes.

## Dual Brush

Moving down we come to the Dual Brush palette, which makes it possible for you to blend two different brushes together. When you open this palette, notice that you are presented with the currently loaded brush presets (Figure 13.37). This blending of the brushes' options will work best with two very different brush types, so pick accordingly. Usually a vary large and fat brush will work well with a brush with higher scatter

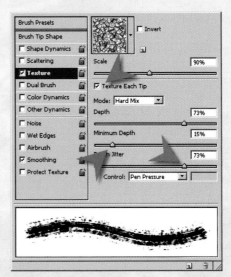

**FIGURE 13.36**   The Texture palette showing the results of adding Depth and Depth Jitter to a brush.

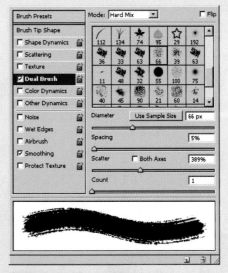

**FIGURE 13.37**   The Dual Brush palette.

settings. Picking the mode of the blend will also have a great effect on the look of the brush. The Diameter, Spacing, Scatter, and Count sliders all affect the chosen brush as they do in the other palettes.

## Color Dynamics

When you're painting in Photoshop the color of the brush is whatever you've set the primary color to. The Color Dynamics palette (Figure 13.38) makes it possible to vary the colors used in your brush. To demonstrate how this works, set the background color to a color of your choice and move the Foreground/Background Jitter slider up to 100%. Leave the default control set to Brush Pressure.

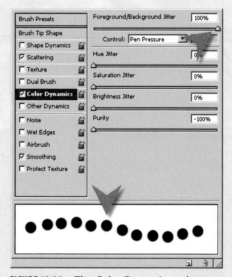

**FIGURE 13.38** The Color Dynamics palette.

Notice that in the preview window nothing has seemed to change. Unfortunately, the preview window does not display the changes in the brush when you change the settings in the Color Dynamics palette. To see the changes you have made to your brush, you will need to make a stroke in your painting or, better yet, in a test image. Figure 13.39 shows an image with a stroke using the settings in Figure 13.38.

What is happening here? Assuming that you chose any color other than white for your background color, shouldn't you be getting a stroke that displays variations between the foreground and background colors and not between black and white? For the user new to the brushes controls, this can be confusing. There is one more slider that must be moved for you to get jitter between the foreground and background colors, and that is the Purity slider. Right now the slider is set to a value of -100. At this setting there is absolutely no pure color in your stroke. Read this as no color at all, just variations of black and white. Move the slider to 0, as shown in Figure 13.40.

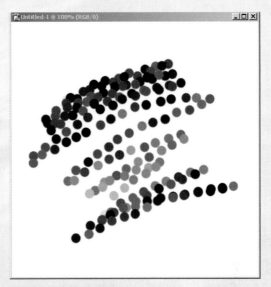

**FIGURE 13.39**   The result of increasing the Foreground/
Background Jitter slider.

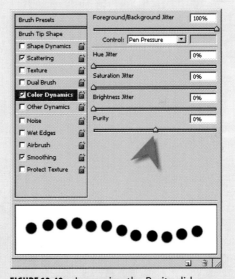

**FIGURE 13.40**   Increasing the Purity slider.

Notice that the preview window does not change. It never will. You
need to once again make a stroke in your test image. Now you should notice that the color of the stroke does indeed vary between the foreground
and background colors, as Figure 13.41 shows.

If the Purity setting of 0 gives you the jitter between the foreground
and background colors, what does increasing the Purity setting to a

**FIGURE 13.41**     The result of moving the Purity slider.

greater value yield? Increasing the Purity value increases the intensity of the color. This increase makes the jitter greater so that it is no longer just between the foreground and background colors but between the foreground and a very intense background variation. Be careful not to raise the Purity setting above 0 if you want to vary only between the foreground and background colors; Figure 13.42 shows what happens when you set it too high.

**FIGURE 13.42**     The resulting stroke when the Purity slider is set too high.

Assuming that you now have your brush set to jitter between the foreground and background colors as you want, you can explore the other sliders. They are, for the most part, self-explanatory, as you can see in Figure 13.43:

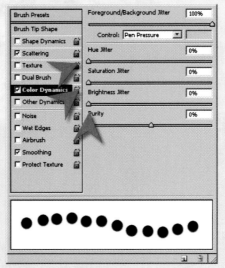

**FIGURE 13.43**    The remaining sliders in the Color Dynamics palette.

- The Hue Jitter slider will change the hue (color) of the background color that the brush jitters to. A low setting and the hue will vary only slightly away from the background color. An extremely high setting will vary hue jitter to a color completely different from the original background color.
- The Saturation Jitter slider will vary the saturation (grayness) of the background color.
- The Brightness Jitter slider will vary the brightness (value) of the background color.

Once again, to see the results of varying these sliders you will need to try out your strokes in a test image as the preview window does not display the color information.

## Other Dynamics

The Other Dynamics palette features controls for two settings we've already discussed. Recall the Opacity and Flow controls in the Options bar that appear when you pick the Brush tool. While these controls adjust the flow and opacity for the stroke overall, the settings in the Other Dynamics palette (Figure 13.44) set the flow and opacity on a dab-by-dab level.

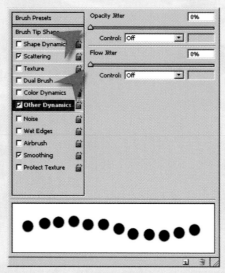

**FIGURE 13.44**   The Other Dynamics palette showing the Opacity and Flow sliders.

Because these settings work on the individual dab in the stroke, they can be used in conjunction with the general Opacity and Flow settings in the Options bar to create almost limitless varieties of effects.

The last five menu items in the Brushes palette (Figure 13.45) do not open their own sub-palettes. Instead, these items are just boxes that can be checked or unchecked as you like. What follows is a description of what each of the check boxes does.

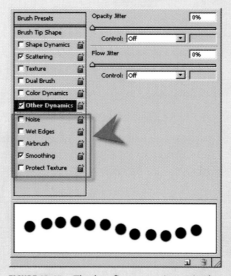

**FIGURE 13.45**   The last five menu items in the Brushes palette.

**Noise:** Checking the Noise box will add a grainy effect to the brush stroke, as Figure 13.46 shows. The effect is most noticeable if the hardness of your stroke is very low.

**Wet Edges:** Checking the Wet Edges box will give you a puddling effect. This in some respects resembles the nonuniform way that watercolor will sometimes dry, as shown in Figure 13.47.

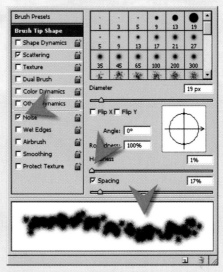

**FIGURE 13.46**    The results of checking the Noise box.

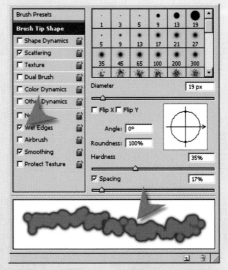

**FIGURE 13.47**    The puddling effect caused by checking the Wet Edges box.

**Airbrush:** This check box, when selected, does the same thing as the Airbrush icon on the Brush Options bar.

**Smoothing:** When the Smoothing option is checked, Photoshop will "smooth" a stroke made by a brush (Figure 13.48). With Smoothing deselected, a brush will sometimes draw small, straight areas when painting a stroke. Notice the arrow pointing to the slight angle visible on the curve with Smoothing unchecked. If you will look closely, you can see several slight angles within the stroke.

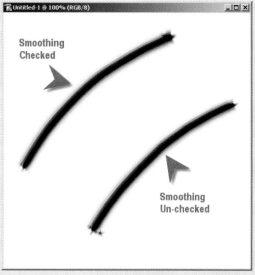

**FIGURE 13.48**    The result of checking the Smoothing box.

**Protect Texture:** This last check box works only with textured brushes and you will see no change in any of the other brushes. When checked, the option applies the same pattern at the same scale to all brushes that paint with a texture. This makes it easy to have a consistent look throughout a painting that uses patterns.

In this already rather lengthy chapter we have explored the Brushes palette and have seen the innumerable ways that the default brushes can be altered to suit your particular needs. This is basic to your understanding of painting within Photoshop. You must know your tool and how to make it behave the way you expect and want. In the following section, we will look at the process of making your own custom brushes and not just altering settings of the default libraries.

## SECTION 3: CREATING YOUR OWN PHOTOSHOP BRUSHES

Why with all the brushes that already ship with Photoshop would anyone want to create their own brushes? The answer to this question is simple. You save custom brushes to do exactly what you want when you want to do it. You could, if you had the time and inclination, re-create a brush or create an entirely new brush every time you painted, but this would indeed be a lengthy and time-consuming way of working. Or suppose you are commissioned to do a series of images that all need to look and feel-similar. Being able to create and save libraries and variants of brushes makes this possible. Fortunately, within Photoshop you do have the ability to create and save brushes and brush libraries. You can create an entire custom set for every project you work on if you care to. In this section we look at creating and organizing your brushes.

### Creating and Saving Brushes in Photoshop

You already have learned how to change the settings of the default brushes to get them to behave like you want by using the brush options. Suppose there is one custom brush that you keep coming back to time and time again. Here is how to save your new brush to the Tools Preset menu.

Click on the Brush Preset Picker icon located on the left of the Tool Options bar. From the menu that opens, click on the small triangle in the circular button on the top left of the menu (Figure 13.49).

This displays a menu loaded with different commands. The top command is New Brush Preset. Click this and a dialog box opens asking you to name your new brush, as shown in Figure 13.50.

Name your brush and click OK. Your newly saved brush now appears at the bottom of the entire list of brushes. It is as simple as that. There is even a small shortcut you can use if you want, and this is displayed on the Brush Preset Picker menu. This time, instead of clicking on the small triangle, click the button that is directly below it. This immediately opens the dialog box shown in Figure 13.51, where you can name your brush and save it.

You may have noticed that there are a lot of additional items on the menu displayed by clicking on the triangle on the Brush Preset Picker (Figure 13.52). For the most part, these commands are self-explanatory, but let's go over them quickly here.

Below the New Brush Preset command are two commands, Rename Brush and Delete Brush, which do just what they say; rename or delete brushes in the preset list.

**FIGURE 13.49**    Click the small triangle on the Brush Preset Picker.

FIGURE 13.50   The New Brush Preset command.

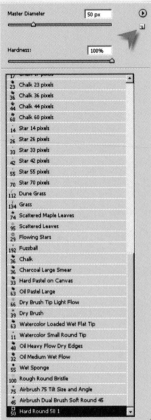

FIGURE 13.51   The Save Brush dialog box.

FIGURE 13.52   All the commands.

The next six commands change the way the brushes are displayed in the Brush Preset picker. The best way to see what they do is to click on them and see what changes.

The next command opens the Preset Manager. Here you can arrange, name, delete, and perform a number of different operations on your brush libraries.

The next four commands do the following: the Reset Brushes command resets the brushes in Photoshop back to the default library and settings; Load Brushes allows you to load additional or custom brush libraries; Save Brushes lets you save all of the currently loaded brushes into a custom library; and Replace Brushes replaces the currently loaded library with a different one. Below those commands, you will see a list of brush libraries currently available to Photoshop.

## CREATING A CUSTOM BRUSH IN PHOTOSHOP USING A PHOTOGRAPHIC TEXTURE

There is another way to create brushes in Photoshop that involves more than just tweaking default brushes. This method involves using images to create an almost endless supply of custom brushes. You can make brushes from photos or scanned images, or you can even draw your own.

This method of creating brushes is unbelievably simple and straightforward. In this section, we will create a brush from a photographic image, though you can use the same procedure for creating a brush from a drawing or anything else you can bring up within Photoshop.

ON THE CD

Generally, you should look for imagery that has good contrasts between the lights and darks. For this example, a photo of tree bark makes the perfect subject (Figure 13.53). The image is included on the CD-ROM.

While it is possible to make a brush as large as you want, for practical painting purposes it is probably best to stick with a brush that is around 200 pixels in the max direction. With the photo of the tree bark opened in Photoshop, resize the image so that the size of the image is 200 pixels in both dimensions, as shown in Figure 13.54.

**FIGURE 13.53**    A photo of tree bark that is perfect for creating a custom brush.

Though you can save a brush that is a combination of any width and height, square-based brushes seem to work very well. Increase the contrast somewhat and convert the image to grayscale, as shown in Figure 13.55.

**FIGURE 13.54**
The resized
texture.

**FIGURE 13.55**    The
image converted
to grayscale and
contrast increased.

At this point you can, if you want, create a brush from this image. Actually, you can create a brush at any step in the process that suits you. To create the brush you simply go into the Edit menu and select Define Brush Preset, as shown in Figure 13.56.

| | |
|---|---|
| Undo New Channel | Ctrl+Z |
| Step Forward | Shift+Ctrl+Z |
| Step Backward | Alt+Ctrl+Z |
| Fade... | Shift+Ctrl+F |
| Cut | Ctrl+X |
| Copy | Ctrl+C |
| Copy Merged | Shift+Ctrl+C |
| Paste | Ctrl+V |
| Paste Into | Shift+Ctrl+V |
| Clear | |
| Check Spelling... | |
| Find and Replace Text... | |
| Fill... | Shift+F5 |
| Stroke... | |
| Free Transform | Ctrl+T |
| Transform | ▶ |
| Define Brush Preset... | |
| Define Pattern... | |
| Define Custom Shape... | |
| Purge | ▶ |
| Color Settings... | Shift+Ctrl+K |
| Keyboard Shortcuts... | Alt+Shift+Ctrl+K |
| Preset Manager... | |
| Preferences | ▶ |

**FIGURE 13.56**    The Define Brush
Preset command.

Your new brush is displayed as a thumbnail in the Brush Name dialog box, shown in Figure 13.57.

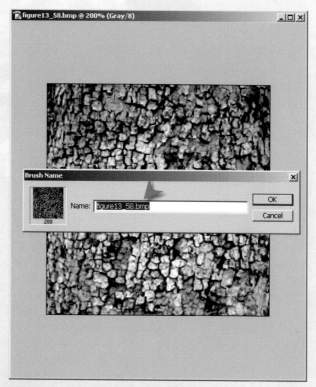

**FIGURE 13.57**    Name your new brush.

Name the brush anything that you would like and click OK. You now have a new brush. The brush is at its rough state at this point. Now it is up to you to go into the brush options and tweak the brush to get it to behave just as you want.

While these steps will provide you with a perfectly usable brush, just the addition of a few more steps will give you a better and more customizable brush, so to continue do the following.

Once you have converted the image to grayscale and adjusted the contrast, to give you an idea of how the brush will look when painting, add an alpha channel under the Channels tab. It does not matter what you call the alpha; the default of "Alpha 1" is just fine.

With the alpha channel active, pick the Gradient Fill tool and fill with a radial gradient using black and white, as shown in Figure 13.58.

Make the original layer active, and load the alpha channel as a selection. You should see marching ants around the middle of the image, as

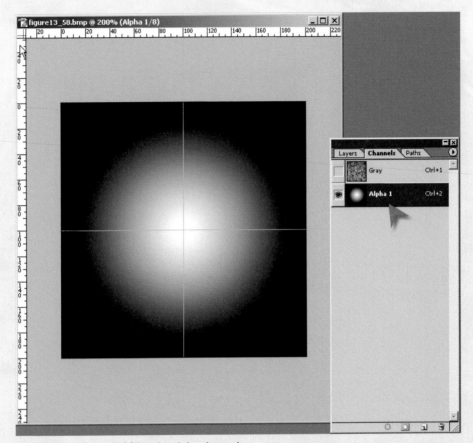

**FIGURE 13.58** The radial fill in the alpha channel.

shown in Figure 13.59. You can see what the marching ants look like very lightly against the image.

Copy, create a new image, and paste into the new image (Figure 13.60).

Now you have a nice image that fades to white on the edges. Go ahead and tweak the contrast if you like. Once again, go to the Edit menu and select the Define Brush Preset command. Name your paper something descriptive and click Yes (Figure 13.61).

ON THE CD

The previous method will work with any image. With experimentation you will find a working method that suits your painting style best. A large number of rough brush libraries are included on the CD-ROM and were created using this procedure.

Now that you have created a number of different brushes, it is time to learn what to do with them. The next section describes how to save and create brush libraries. Use the following instructions and you will soon have a vast number of organized brush libraries that you can share with anyone who uses Photoshop.

**FIGURE 13.59**　The alpha channel loaded as a selection.

**FIGURE 13.60**　A new image created by pasting from the Clipboard.

## Creating Brush Libraries of Your Custom Brushes

Assuming that you have created a number of new brushes and saved them, there is one last thing that you will want to do: create a library of your new brushes. The reason that you would want to do this is simple.

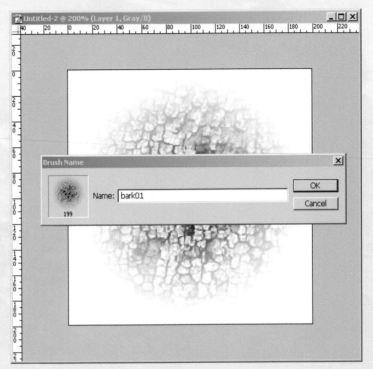

**FIGURE 13.61** Saving your new brush.

Should you ever by accident (or intentionally) reset your brushes back to their default setting and if you have not saved all your custom brushes into another library, they will be lost.

It is very simple to save your own brushes, and you should do it regularly. Just select the Save Brushes command from the Brush Presets menu, as shown in Figure 13.62.

This opens a dialog box asking you what to call your new library and gives you the chance to save your library to any location on your computer, as shown in Figure 13.63.

It is easiest to save to the default location so Photoshop always knows where to find your new brushes. Once you have saved your new brush library, you will want to open the Preset Manager (Figure 13.64). Here you can delete any brushes you may not want, rename, and click and drag the brush icons to rearrange the brushes.

There are several very good books that can take you deeper into Photoshop's brushes if you care to find out more information, but these few and simple steps will fill most all of your brush needs.

In this lengthy section, you have learned about Photoshop's powerful brush engine. You have learned how to tweak the default brushes to get them to behave for your particular painting style, how to create custom

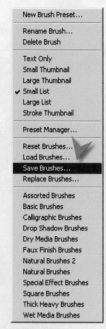

**FIGURE 13.62**   The Save Brushes command.

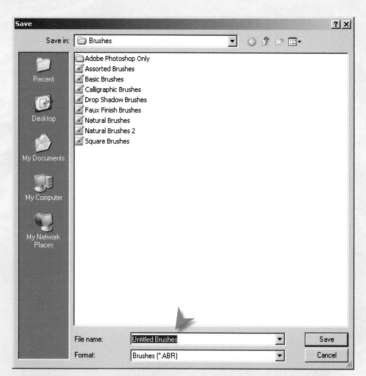

**FIGURE 13.63**   Saving a brush library.

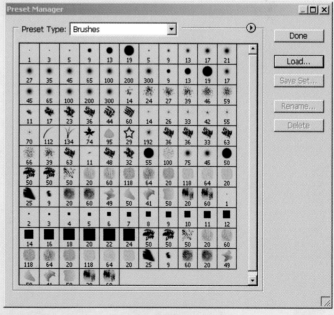

**FIGURE 13.64**   The Brush Preset Manager.

brushes from images, how to save brushes, and organize them into your own personal libraries. Beware that sometimes creating new and innovative brushes becomes almost as much fun as the actual painting.

## CONCLUSION

Now we move on to Part III of our book: tutorials covering different subject matter. The first tutorial will cover painting eyes. After all, in a book on character design and digital painting, what better place to start than with the windows to the soul.

# DIGITAL PAINTING: BRINGING IT ALL TOGETHER

This section contains tutorials on how to approach different subject matter. By no means do these tutorials show the only, or even the best, way of approaching different subjects. They show only one way to approach the subject. This book is about character design, so the majority of the tutorials and demonstrations in this section are figurative in nature.

In Part III, the following assumptions have been made:

**You already have a basic working knowledge of Photoshop.** When we talk about different commands and effects, it is assumed that you know what we are talking about. In addition, most chapters in Part III have a little section called "What You Need to Know About Photoshop for This Chapter" that further outlines what you are expected to know.

**You, the reader and artist, should do your own interpretation of the steps taken here.** It would be much more preferable for you to experiment as you are following along.

**At this point in the book, you need more graphics and less explanation.** The chapters in this section are very heavy on graphics and lighter on text than the beginning demonstrations. Most artists would rather look at step-by-step images with brief explanations as opposed to long-winded paragraphs that attempt to explain a visual concept. After all, isn't one picture worth a thousand words?

You will notice in these demonstrations that the author often changes his mind about what he's doing, which is both a fault and a blessing. A firm idea almost always comes to mind, but then often something not previously considered pops up, changing the direction of the work.

ON THE CD

If a custom texture or brush has not been mentioned before in the book and is used for the first time in this section, it will be included in the relevant chapter's folder on the CD-ROM.

Photoshop has been used for all images. Much of what you see here is also applicable to other programs, but if you use Photoshop, it will be easier for you to duplicate the steps.

# PAINTING AN EYE

This chapter covers one of the basic skills needed when you are painting characters: painting a realistic eye. Painting the features of a face is not as hard as it sometimes seems. In this chapter, you will learn a simple way to paint a human eye. This method, as with most of the demonstrations in this book, is applicable to just about any type of eye that you may need to paint.

## What You Need to Know About Photoshop for This Chapter

This tutorial assumes that you know some fundamentals of working in Photoshop, such as:

- Where individual palettes are located. In this specific tutorial, we will not be changing very many of Photoshop's defaults.
- How to adjust a brush's opacity.
- How to resize your brush and sample color from within the image (using hot keys).

You can arrange Photoshop's workspace to suit your own liking, so this chapter does not discuss where to locate specific items.

Once again, always remember when you are painting on the computer to save your files. Make it a habit to save numerically named versions of your work. One of the best things about digital painting is this ability to save multiple versions that you can revert to if you make a major mistake.

**TUTORIAL**    **Painting the Window into a Character's Soul, the Eye**

In this tutorial, we aren't doing any preliminary drawing or scanning sketches; however, if doing so makes you more comfortable, feel free to scan in a sketch or drawing that you have done. To paint an eye, follow these steps:

1. Start Photoshop and create a new image document (600 × 600 pixels is a good size). Make sure that the white of the image is covered. Either create the image with a colored paper or fill the canvas with a light-gray color.
2. Select the Airbrush Pen Opacity Flow brush. (This brush is a default Photoshop brush; if you do not see it in your Brushes palette, reset your brushes.)
3. You need to make one change to the default brush before you begin drawing your eye. In the Brush Tip Shape palette, change the hardness to about 50%, as shown in Figure 14.1. By changing these settings, you create a brush that looks slightly softer along the edges as

you draw. This brush also tends to produce a softer gray if you press lightly on your stylus and becomes darker as you press harder. This is a great way to work because your initial strokes are light, and as you refine your drawing, you can press harder to make the strokes darker.

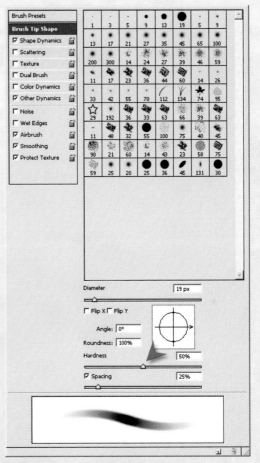

**FIGURE 14.1**    Brush settings for drawing the eye.

4. Set your brush's color to a mid-value gray, set the opacity to about 30% and the size to around 10, and then begin drawing an eye. As you draw, remember that the eye is basically spherical in shape and is surrounded by the fleshy folds of the eyelids. While drawing, you must always remember the three-dimensional aspects of your subject, or your images will look flat and lifeless. Your initial sketch should look something like Figure 14.2.

5. Continue drawing until you have a fairly representational eye, as shown in Figure 14.3.

**FIGURE 14.2**    Beginning the drawing.

**FIGURE 14.3**    Continuing to draw the eye.

6. Let's add a little color to the sketch. From the Filters menu, choose Render, and then click Lighting Effects. Add an omni light right about the iris of the eye. Change the color of the light to some nice fleshy color. Move the Brightness slider down so that all the color is not washed out to white. Once you apply the effect, your image should look something like Figure 14.4.

**FIGURE 14.4**    Lighting effect applied to the sketch of the eye.

7. Switch to the Airbrush Soft Round brush. Set the Opacity slider to a fairly low value of between 20% and 40%. From the Color palette, select a dark orange color to represent the dark flesh color and begin painting in the shadow areas of the eye, as shown in Figure 14.5. Do not worry about "staying in the lines"; just concentrate on getting color down. Do not paint too opaquely or you will lose your underlying image. Switch back to your original brush and paint in some of

**FIGURE 14.5**    Painting in the shadow areas and the iris's color.

the iris's color. Notice that the colors used in Figure 14.5 are not intense. A painting of uniform, bright intensity is very tiring on the eye.

8. Select your original brush again if you have changed back and forth to the Airbrush, and start redrawing any of the eye that was painted over too opaquely. Begin to add in more detail and brighter color, as shown in Figure 14.6.

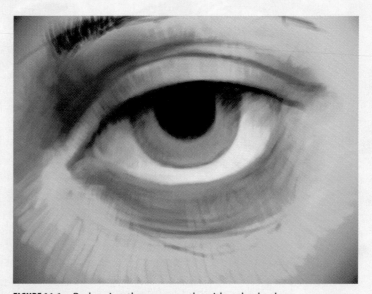

**FIGURE 14.6**   Redrawing the eye over the airbrushed colors.

9. Start to work some lighter color into the image. Notice in Figure 14.7 that as the eye is painted, deep reds and subtle pinks have been put in the corners and lower lids, that the hazel color of the iris is not intense, and that the white of the eye is anything but white. Also notice the amount of red that is in the deepest shadow areas. Try to use deep reds instead of blacks when drawing the darkest areas. Black will kill the life of the image, whereas deep red will add life to it. Do not worry that the strokes are looking rough at this point.

10. Continue to add more color. Do not get too intense, but do get brighter. In Figure 14.8, some greens and browns have been added to the iris, the white of the eye has been lightened, and some lighter flesh tones have been added around the eye. Also notice that highlights are being added. Because an eye's surface is wet, the highlights are very sharp and shiny. The edges need to be relatively crisp and lean slightly toward the color of the light source. All of this work is done using the original brush while varying the size and opacity where needed.

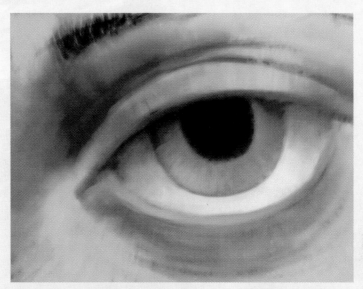

**FIGURE 14.7**    Working lighter colors into the eye painting.

**FIGURE 14.8**    Adding more color to the iris of the eye.

11. By now, your eye looks pretty good, though it is somewhat messy. Let's clean it up some, as has been done in Figure 14.9. Use the blending method described in Chapter 11 and begin to smooth out some of the rough strokes. Remember that you are not trying to obliterate the strokes but simply soften them a touch. The last thing to do is add back some of the detail that has been blended out. Switch back to

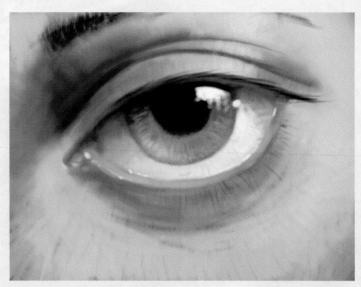

**FIGURE 14.9** Slight blending and reestablishing the detail to finish the eye.

your original brush and redraw some of the small detail in the creases and lids of the eyes that may have been lost in the blending process, add a few eyelashes, and you are done, as shown in Figure 14.9.

## CONCLUSION

Well, that is about all there is to painting an eye. You can use this general technique when painting virtually any eye on any character. Put a lot of time and practice into painting eyes. They are one of the most important features in a face and the one that grabs most of our attention when we are interacting with each other. In the next chapter, we will expand on what we have learned and concentrate on painting the entire face.

# PAINTING A FACE

A face may be one of the most difficult subject matters that an artist tackles. In this chapter, we will paint a human face. The techniques presented here are pretty much applicable to painting any sort of face, be it human or alien.

| TUTORIAL | GENERAL WORKING METHODS THAT YOU MAY WANT TO USE WHEN PAINTING A FACE |

Here is one method you can use to realize a full-color, digitally painted face and head. Just follow these steps:

1. Start by making a sketch, as shown in Figure 15.1. You can draw it by using either the traditional paper-and-pencil method or drawing directly on the computer; it really does not matter. If you start with a pencil sketch, you will, of course, need to scan the image into your computer. At this stage, you should consider resolution issues, along with what the final output will be. Will your image be used for print or on the Web? A print image will need to be at a much higher resolution than a Web image. When starting with the scan, consider working with an image that has a resolution of 200 dpi and that is grayscale. A 200-dpi resolution is large enough to let you include all the necessary facial details, is high enough resolution to print well, and is small enough as far as memory requirements to allow you to paint quickly. If you are going to be drawing directly on the computer, make sure that your output resolution is set when you create the image. Most of the imagery you will paint will probably start at fewer than 1,500 pixels in the largest dimension.

2. Once you have set your resolution and have a basic design ready, you are ready to move on. A pencil-sketch scan usually contains a large range of gray values as will a sketch drawn directly within the program. In this particular case the drawing paper had numerous small, colored flecks. These types of things left in the sketch can be distracting and should be made less distinct if not eliminated. If not much variation exists between the strokes that you are drawing with or in your scan (i.e., the sketch is predominantly black and white), you may want to skip this step. If the sketch contains lots of distracting marks and you want to remove them, use the Levels command (Image > Adjustments > Levels). Use this command to reduce the number of gray values while leaving the image looking cleaner without the speckles, as shown in Figure 15.2.

3. Save your file—we cannot emphasize this step enough. Make it a habit to save numerically named versions of your work. One of the best things about digital painting is this ability to save multiple versions to which you can revert if you make a major mistake.

4. Cut and paste the image back into the original.

FIGURE 15.1    The beginning sketch.

FIGURE 15.2    The sketch after we used the Levels command.

5. Set the Composite Blending mode to Multiply, as shown in Figure 15.3. This provides a top layer where the white has become transparent, allowing you to paint on the background layer while showing the original sketch through the top layer.

6. As a general rule, it is not recommended that you paint on a white background. The reason for this is simple. Against a white background, especially on the computer monitor, virtually every color and value will look too dark. Therefore, you should always add a tone of color to the background of the image. In Photoshop, fill the background layer with either a color or a gray value, as shown in Figure 15.4. We chose the color in this case to contrast with later colors that will be added as we paint. You could add a gradation if you prefer.

**FIGURE 15.3**  Converting the layer's Blending mode to Multiply.

7. Create a new layer for this next step. In Figure 15.5, a violet color has been added into the turban area on the new layer. Always, when painting an image with a substantial amount of skin, begin by painting in some of the surrounding colors. These colors will influence the choices you will make as you pick colors for the skin areas. The reason for painting on a new layer will become apparent should you need to make corrections later in the painting. It is much easier to fix errors if the main elements of your painting are separate entities.

**FIGURE 15.4**    Adding color to the background.

**FIGURE 15.5**    Painting color into the turban.

Most of the painting in this image is done using only two or three brushes. The main brush used is the default brush, Airbrush Pen Opacity Flow. We tweaked the size and settings of the brush slightly as needed.

8. Create another new layer, as shown in Figure 15.6, and begin adding the skin colors. You must go to the Color palette and actually select the individual colors that you want to use because the image contains limited colors. At this point, experiment with finding colors that you actually want to use. Begin by picking the darkest colors of the skin and blocking in the whole shape of the face. Doing so will help you establish the value range of your image. Do not concentrate on laying color down only on the figure. Work all over the image in these early stages to maintain the color theme.

**FIGURE 15.6**     Painting in the large dark shape of the face.

9. In Figure 15.7, the planes of the face are being carefully developed as you refine and add lighter colors to the face. You do not need to try and blend the color at this time. Let the overlapping edges of the brush strokes be the areas where you sample the colors you paint with.

10. Notice in the closeup of the painting in Figure 15.8 that some of the underlying background color shows through the skin colors that are being painted. This is particularly apparent in the temple area of the head. Try to get some of your background colors into the figure and,

**FIGURE 15.7**    Defining the planes in the face using lighter colors.

if possible, some of your foreground colors into the background. Do not be concerned with "staying within the lines." Notice in Figure 15.8, particularly within the circled area, the high saturation of the colors in the flesh. Notice too, that the purple is reminiscent of the color of the turban. This is the reason you paint the colors surrounding the skin at the beginning.

11. Begin sampling some of the colors within the image itself using the Eyedropper tool and painting with those sampled colors. (Photoshop's hot key for the Eyedropper tool is Alt; using the hot key makes it very fast to sample and go back to painting.) You will still need to go to the Color palette for some colors, but more and more you can simply sample colors that are being created within the painting.

**FIGURE 15.8** Notice the intense color and the different colors in the face, as you can see in the circled area.

12. At this point you can merge the sketch layer and the layer you are painting the skin color on. Continue to refine the drawing while painting in more detail and gradually covering the sketch. Figure 15.9 shows a closeup of the face. Notice that you can see some of the sketch only in smaller areas as it is covered in the painting process. This is most noticeable around the mouth.

**FIGURE 15.9** The merging of the sketch and painting layers.

13. Figure 15.10 shows the entire painting and how the features are being refined and developed. Notice how simply the eye is painted. There is no need at all to paint every eyelash. Also be aware of the subtle but noticeable color change in the corner of the eye. If you simply use a dark brown or black for all of your darks, you will end up with an image that looks dead. Notice the highlights that are being developed on the skin, particularly on the tip of the nose and the eye; this is where the background color is now being integrated into the overall skin color in a most dramatic fashion. This is just a matter of using the background color as the highlight. In dark-skinned people, the highlights on the skin are generally much more specular and shiny than in people with light or pale skin.

**FIGURE 15.10**    The background color being used as the highlight color.

14. Using the same brush, continue to paint the rest of the head. As you can see in Figure 15.11, you gradually and ever so slightly cool the warmer colors of the face using the blue green of the background. The shadows of the figure vary from warm to cool. Varying the colors of the shadows will keep the figure looking alive. Work your strokes across the form, meaning that the strokes are perpendicular to the long axis of the body part being painted.

**FIGURE 15.11**    Refining the painting and cooling the colors in the flesh using the background color.

15. The underlying sketch is just about painted over completely by this time. Continue smoothing and refining the face, adding highlights where appropriate and blocking in some color in the background and

shirt area. Remember, the highlights should take on the cast of the surrounding color (or, in this case, a slight blue). Some serious consideration now needs to be given to the background and collar area of the painting. The background is a combination of flesh tones mixed with the background color and some blue/purples to bring in some of the turban color. Begin to establish the shadow patterns within the turban, separating the light side from the dark side. The shirt is painted in golden tones. This is not by chance; these golden tones are picked to enhance the colors in the face and contrast the purple turban, as shown in Figure 15.12.

**FIGURE 15.12**  Adding the background, shirt, and the value patterns within the turban.

16. Figure 15.13 shows a closeup of the face so you can see all the color and general simplicity of the brush strokes used to paint.

**FIGURE 15.13**   A closeup of the face

17. Additional work is now concentrated on the turban (see Figure 15.14). Merge the turban layer. Using the same brush, refine the lights and darks and cover the sketch as you build up the color.

18. In Figure 15.15, you are pretty much finished with painting the face. You should now have the background painted. The turban is painted with enough detail that the viewer will understand what it is yet it will not compete with the face for attention. For this study, the shirt will remain just roughed in.

19. The portrait needs one more thing to make it more intriguing and that is some jewelry. Create a new layer and paint a pair of earrings on your figure. Do not overstate them as you want them to add interest to the face and not compete for the viewer's attention. Save your file and you are done, as you can see in Figure 15.16.

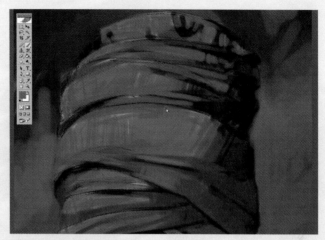

**FIGURE 15.14**    Painting the turban.

**FIGURE 15.15**    The finished face.

**FIGURE 15.16**   The finished face with earrings.

## CONCLUSION

That's about it for painting a face. Remember to work at low-opacity settings so that the colors can build themselves slowly and with subtle transitions. The procedures you have learned here are applicable to virtually any type of face, from alien to any human face that you can imagine. In the next chapter, we will paint long, dark hair.

# PAINTING HAIR

Hair is not as hard to paint as it may seem. This chapter will show you how to paint one type of hair. Because it is difficult to paint just hair without painting a face, this chapter will also review the basics of painting a face. The secret to success for painting hair is to not get caught up in all of the small details, namely the individual strands of hair. Hair is usually simple variations of the skin's colors. Stay away from using too much yellow when painting blond hair. Instead, use lots of yellowish grays with muted browns and with touches of yellow in the highlights. Red hair has lots of oranges and purples in the light areas. The highlights on black hair often appear bluish. The same is true for dark brown hair but not to the same degree. In this chapter, darker brown hair will be painted being lit from both the side and with a strong backlight.

## WHAT YOU NEED TO KNOW ABOUT PHOTOSHOP FOR THIS CHAPTER

For this chapter, the special things you need to know about Photoshop are

- Where individual palettes are located
- How to create and manipulate individual layers
- How to adjust a brush's opacity
- How to resize your brush and sample color from within the image (preferably using hot keys)

**TUTORIAL**    ## A TECHNIQUE FOR PAINTING LONG, DARK HAIR

The best process is to paint both the hair and the face at the same time, but for the sake of this tutorial, we will work up the face quickly and put most of our emphasis on the hair. Figure 16.1 shows the most basic sketch done in Photoshop. You could of course do the initial sketch and scan in your image to work on. This image is only meant to establish the position of the figure and the general areas that will be light and dark.

When you have your sketch in Photoshop either by scanning or drawing within the program itself, take some time and refine the image a bit more. There is an inherent danger here. You want to refine the sketch to become more familiar with your subject, but you do not want to get a drawing that is so finished all you do is a digital coloring book exercise. In particular, with this exercise we want to show the patterns within the hair that will be painted. Always when painting you must be willing to make changes and or corrections to your work. Figure 16.2 shows the sketch that has been developed a bit further.

At this point the fun begins. The first thing to do is to get rid of all the white in the background. You will remember, as mentioned earlier, that

**FIGURE 16.1**    The basic figure sketch we will be working from.

**FIGURE 16.2**    The sketch in a more refined state showing the patterns in the hair.

this is the most important initial step. If you paint on a white background, all of your colors will look too dark.

1. Select the entire image and copy and paste it back into the canvas. This will leave you with a sketch on the canvas for the background and a duplicate drawing on a new layer. Change the blending mode of the layer to Multiply. This will turn all the white areas transparent while leaving the sketch visible. Make the background layer active and from the Filter menu, select Render > Lighting Effects. In this particular case, two lights are applied to the background image. The top is a warm color and the bottom is cooler. Figure 16.3 shows the sketch with the lighting effect applied.

**FIGURE 16.3** Applying the lighting filter to the background layer of the painting.

2. Remember to save your file at this point. We cannot emphasize enough that you must always remember to save your files. Make it a habit to save numerically named versions of your work. One of the best things about digital painting is this ability to save multiple versions that you can revert to if you make a major mistake.

3. Begin to block in the darker areas of both the face and hair. Always try to establish your value patterns as early in the painting process as possible. Work on the dark colors of the face and on the dark colors in the hair using the same color and brush. In this particular case, use an enlarged version of the Airbrush Pen Opacity Flow brush. It is best to work on the skin and the hair concurrently so that both develop in visual continuity. Figure 16.4 shows the process of filling in the darker areas of the painting. Notice that there is not a lot of concern for "staying in the lines."

**FIGURE 16.4**    Beginning the initial block in of the darker areas in the painting.

4. We will be using the Airbrush Pen Opacity Flow brush for the majority of the work in both the hair and skin. Continue painting in the darker colors of the hair and skin, as shown in Figure 16.5. Set the size of the brush to about twice as large as you think you need it. This will prevent you from going in and drawing all of the small details. The goal at this stage of the painting is to get the larger value patterns painted in; we're not concerned about the small individual strokes. Also at this point, begin to develop some of the color within the background.

5. The steps we've done up to this point are only concerned with value. Now we will begin to concentrate on color. This involves adding color to both the skin areas and the hair. Notice that most of the colors that are in the skin are also used in the hair with only value changes apparent. Save the image. Continue to work additional colors into the background. At some point you will be adding some of the background colors into the foreground and vice versa, as shown in Figure 16.6.

**FIGURE 16.5** Getting all the darker color and value into the hair and face and the start of work in the background.

**FIGURE 16.6** Adding color into the figure, hair, and background.

6. Sampling color from the lighter areas of the hair and then lightening it slightly in the Color palette, paint in some light touches into lighter side of the hair. Darken and reestablish the darker areas in both the face and the hair, as shown in Figure 16.7.

7. Using the same brush but setting it with slightly more opacity, paint in the general hair color over the whole of the head, as shown in Figure 16.8. Do not paint in individual strands of hair, and try not to cover the forms in the hair that you have developed in the earlier steps.

**FIGURE 16.7** Painting some lighter and darker touches into all of the hair and skin.

**FIGURE 16.8** Painting in the general, overall color of the hair.

8. Now switch back and forth between some lighter and darker colors to reestablish and clean up the edges of the hair. Sample some of the light bluish-gray color from the background and paint highlights into the hair. Also paint and tweak some of the smaller details in both the hair and face that you have not been as concerned with up to this point. Add more color and work in to the background, as shown in Figure 16.9.

9. Begin to refine areas of the hair. In this case, we're working on the front strand of hair that is hanging over the forehead. Use a slightly smaller brush but not too small because it is still too early to be adding individual strands (Figure 16.10). As you can see, some work needs to be done in the skin areas, specifically in the chest area where the hair covers the skin.

10. The hair needs more dark color. Because you do not want to ruin any of the work you have already done, create a new layer to do this painting on. If you are not satisfied with your results, you can always delete the layer. If you are happy with the results, you can merge the two layers. Figure 16.11 shows the darkened hair on a new layer.

**FIGURE 16.9** Adding some highlights into the hair using background colors.

**FIGURE 16.10** Painting on the front strand of hair hanging over the forehead.

11. In this particular painting the head is strongly backlit. This means that there is a light source behind and, in this case, slightly above the subject. Because of this lighting arrangement, strong highlights will appear on the hair on the top and to the back of the head. A critical thing to remember when painting hair is that it is shiny. Individual strands of hair, though shiny, will not reflect enough light to make a difference; however, when hair is massed together, all the small highlights will group together and form large, dramatically lit areas. Things that are shiny in a painting will reflect the colors of the surrounding environment. In this painting, the highlights in the hair are painted using the light colors of the background. Figure 16.12 shows the highlights strongest toward the backlight and slightly smaller as you come forward on the top of the head.

12. As the hair becomes more refined, add smaller strands. Continue to work both the hair and the skin in the chest area where the two meet. Though this tutorial is not about painting costume or clothing, go ahead and add the shadow areas in the drapery covering the model's body, as shown in Figure 16.13.

**FIGURE 16.11**  Create a new layer and darken the hair.

**FIGURE 16.12**  Adding dramatic highlights into the hair using background colors.

13. More work is done in the area of the drapery by adding the lighter areas. Also, include additional painting in the chest and hair, as shown in Figure 16.14.

14. Occasionally, you may find that you want to increase the richness of the appearance of the colors that you are painting with. An easy way to accomplish this is to select your image, copy it, paste it back onto itself, and change the Blending mode to Multiply. This initially leaves a very dark image but by adjusting the Opacity slider, you will be able to get a slightly darker but much richer-looking painting. When you have the amount of change you want, save the file in case something goes wrong and then merge the two layers. Save your work again. Figure 16.15 shows the result of this process. The image is slightly darker and richer looking.

15. Using the same brush you have been using, begin to clean up the contours of the figure and hair. Also, blend the colors both in the figure and the drapery, as shown in Figure 16.16.

**FIGURE 16.13**    Adding smaller strands of hair, working the areas where the hair and skin overlap, and painting the shadows in the drapery.

**FIGURE 16.14**    More work in both the drapery and skin/hair.

16. Refine the painting in additional areas. In this case, significant work was done to paint the arms and where they meet the hair, as you can see in Figure 16.17.

17. The hair has gotten somewhat flat by this point in the painting. Never be afraid to make changes at any point in the painting process to make the image stronger. Darks are reestablished into the hair to create a greater sense of the form.

18. Now and only now is the time to add some individual strands of hair if you want. By now, the major planes and forms of the hair are painted and unless you go overboard, adding a few individual small details will not harm the image. Be careful, though, not to add light hair into the darker areas and vice versa. Doing so will begin to flatten the form and add visual holes to the image. The majority of the work in this image is done where the hair covers the chest and top of the drapery, as shown in Figure 16.19.

**FIGURE 16.15**    The result of copying, pasting, changing the blending mode, and merging the two layers of the figure.

**FIGURE 16.16**    Cleaning up the figure's contours and blending colors in both the skin and drapery.

**FIGURE 16.17**    Cleaning up the painting in the arms.

**FIGURE 16.18**    Strong darks are painted back into the hair.

**FIGURE 16.19** Adding some individual and detailed strands of hair to the painting.

**FIGURE 16.20** The background is painted using custom brushes.

19. The last thing we need to do is work on the background so that it has some finish to it. Abstract (as in this case) or something a bit more realistic, it does not matter as long as you handle the background with the same care as you use for the main figure. In this stage the background has been painted using custom brushes. These brushes are available on the CD-ROM. After the background is painted, paint a few wisps of hair on the sides of the head overlapping the background to achieve that finished look, as shown in Figure 16.20.

ON THE CD

## CONCLUSION

Now wasn't that simple? The steps we just followed were meant to show a very simple way of painting one kind of hair. As you know, there are as many different types of hair as there are people. Add to the equation that many colors of hair are not natural and a whole book could be written on just painting hair. However, if you remember the simple theory behind the process, any style of hair will be easier to paint. In the next chapter, we will again paint a face but with a difference. Instead of painting a face with a flawless complexion, we will paint one that has many small imperfections, more like in the real world.

# PAINTING A MALE PORTRAIT USING VARIED TEXTURES

You may be wondering why we're devoting so much time to painting with textures. Well, one of the biggest complaints you hear about digital art is that it looks too slick, that it is so perfect it has no soul or life. While the main goal of the remaining chapters of this book is to show various methods of painting different types of characters, they also aim to show that digital art need not be sterile. The goal is not to try to emulate traditional techniques but just possibly to invent a new type of image that while obviously digital in execution is not boring to look at.

*This chapter builds on the things learned in the previous chapters. The basic information that was presented there will not be repeated here.*

## WHAT YOU NEED TO KNOW ABOUT PHOTOSHOP FOR THIS CHAPTER

The following tutorial assumes that you know some fundamentals of working in Photoshop CS or previous versions of Photoshop. You should know such things as

- Where individual palettes are located
- How to create, save, and use patterns
- How to adjust a brush's opacity
- What a layer style is and how to use it
- How to create layers and change their composite method
- How to resize your brush and sample color from within the image (preferably using hot keys)

**TUTORIAL**

*ON THE CD*

## PAINTING A FACE USING LOTS OF TEXTURES

When you're ready to start painting the portrait, follow these steps:

1. Open Photoshop and create a new image file or open a scanned image. The original image painted for this chapter was sketched in pencil, scanned in at 300 dpi, resulting in an image 2100 pixels wide by 2661 pixels high. This sketch (Figure 17.1) is on the CD-ROM if you want to use it as the basis for your painting.
2. Copy and paste the sketch back into the image. Change the blend mode of the newly created layer to darken and temporarily hide this layer by clicking on the eye icon next to it. Change back to the background layer and choose Filter > Render > Lighting Effects to get rid of all of the very bright white in the image, as shown in Figure 17.2. A bluish lighting scheme was chosen.

FIGURE 17.1    The initial sketch scanned into the computer.

FIGURE 17.2    The initial sketch with a bluish lighting effect applied.

ON THE CD

3. Switch back to the hidden layer. Click the eye to unhide the layer, and double-click on the layer to bring up the Layer Style window. Check the Pattern Overlay box. In the area where the thumbnail of the pattern is visible, select a pattern of your choice to be applied to the layer. The pattern used for this tutorial is included on the CD-ROM. Make sure that the blend mode is set to Multiply so that you can see your sketch through the pattern and lower the opacity to something around 65%. Of course, feel free to experiment to get a look that you like, and when you're satisfied, click OK. Figure 17.3 shows the Layer Style window with the settings we used.

4. Figure 17.4 shows the image with the top layer, the layer style applied, and blend mode set to Darken over the bluish background layer. When we are happy with the look, we merge the layer down. For the remainder of the painting, we will be painting directly on the background layer.

5. As when you paint with traditional tools, start by laying in some of the darks first, as shown in Figure 17.5, and then working toward the lighter colors. Airbrush Pen Opacity Flow is a good brush to use in varying sizes and opacities. Use a brush that is about twice as large as you think you need. This will keep you from fussing over the details. Your first goal should always be to establish a strong value statement.

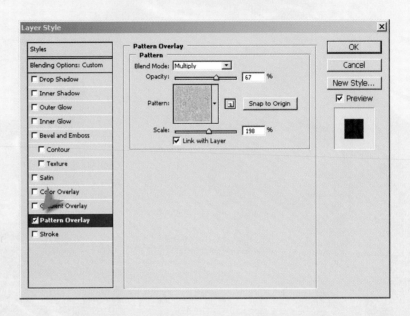

**FIGURE 17.3** The Layer Style window.

**FIGURE 17.4** The image with both layers visible.

**FIGURE 17.5**    Beginning to block in the colors working from dark to light.

6. Continue to fill in and refine the colors still using a large brush (Figure 17.6). You might want to increase the opacity as you work. The opacity of the brush has been increased to about 60%. Do not neglect to work some color into the background as you are painting the face. Go ahead and add some smaller details in a rough fashion. Notice the eye now has some color in the iris.

7. Switch brushes to something with a little texture in it (Figure 17.7). In this case the brush is meant to imitate using pastel or chalk. Continue to paint the colors of the face and the background. This brush and the others used in this tutorial are available on the CD-ROM.

ON THE CD

8. Figure 17.8 shows a closeup of the face so that the textures being used are very apparent.

9. Still using the textured brush, paint some of the skin colors into the background, as shown in Figure 17.9. Painting background color into the foreground, and vice versa, will help maintain a color harmony that is sometimes hard to achieve otherwise. Remember not to get into the coloring-book mindset by just filling in your original lines. A painting is a fluid creation, and you will be much more successful in your efforts if you don't try to fill in your own lines. Your lines are probably wrong anyway.

**FIGURE 17.6** Continuing to add color in the face and the background.

**FIGURE 17.7** Painting with a textured brush.

**FIGURE 17.8** A closeup of the face.

**FIGURE 17.9**    Adding some of the flesh tones into the background.

10. The image now is in what can affectionately be called the "ugly stage." Almost all artists have their images go through this stage. It usually starts when you are about 17 percent into the painting and lasts almost to the end. We are mentioning this seemingly silly point for a serious reason: about this time, we might start looking at our image and tell ourselves that it will never get any better. We may be greatly tempted to simply give up and start over. Don't do that. Remember that everyone you respect as an artist goes through the same thing that you are feeling. Continue painting. If you don't, you will never finish anything and as a consequence will never improve much. Look at Figure 17.10 and notice the eye has been cut pasted and scaled. It was drawn completely wrong; in fact, notice just generally how bad things are looking. Nevertheless, we'll continue to add more detail into the eyes and face, and try to gradually correct some of the additional drawing problems.

11. In Figure 17.11, we are still using the texture brushes and are seriously trying to cover some of the flesh tones and correct some of the drawing errors by copying, pasting, and scaling the pasted section.

**FIGURE 17.10**    The ugly stage has begun, but keep painting and correcting the errors.

**FIGURE 17.11**    Correcting the size of the nose.

When we are happy with the size of the correction, we merge the layers. Notice that the forehead has been slightly lowered and the nose made smaller. The corrections to the painting around the nose have not been made yet. Never be afraid to make a change to improve the picture.

12. Continue to refine the painting in the face using a smaller size brush and start to paint in more of the costume, as you can see in Figure 17.12.

13. With a small brush, start to paint in the beard, as shown in Figure 17.13.

14. The painting is looking a little pale. To correct this, copy the entire image, paste it back into itself, and change the blend mode to Multiply. The image is very dark at this point. It is, in fact, way too dark, so move the Opacity slider down until you get a slightly darker and much richer-looking image. Merge the layer down onto the background or flatten the image, as shown in Figure 17.14.

15. In Figure 17.15, we have some definite drawing problems and we're still fighting the size of the eyes, but we're starting to think that maybe we can save this one. We copy and paste the eye again, and the scale is slightly smaller in the width.

**FIGURE 17.12**    Using a smaller brush to paint in more of the face and to paint the costume.

**FIGURE 17.13**    Painting the beard.

**FIGURE 17.14**    The result of copying, pasting, changing the blend mode to Multiply, adjusting the opacity, and merging the layer down.

**FIGURE 17.15**    Scaling the eye again.

16. Blend some of the textures in the face and paint more texture into the background. Also, we can paint the zipper on the jacket at this point. Paint a few more details into the hair using a smaller brush, as shown in Figure 17.16.
17. As shown in Figure 17.17, repaint the strand of hair that hangs over the forehead and in front of the ear.
18. A shadow is added under the curl, as Figure 17.18 shows. The image is looking as we had hoped. A significant amount of work is done in the background and the image is basically finished.
19. Just for fun, we superimposed the sketch over the finished painting to see how close we remained to our original idea, as shown in Figure 17.19. 🐾

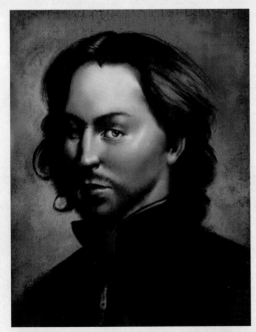

**FIGURE 17.16** Adding the highlight areas into the hair, painting the zipper, and blending some of the face.

**FIGURE 17.17** Painting in the hair curls.

**FIGURE 17.18**   A shadow under the curl.

**FIGURE 17.19**   The sketch superimposed over the painting.

## CONCLUSION

As you can see from the final image, we have created a piece of digital art that does not scream digital when you are viewing it. At the same time, it does not mimic traditional mediums. It is something completely different. If you wisely and judiciously use textures in conjunction with good art skills, you will increase the beauty of your paintings. In the next chapter, we will take a slight detour. Often we get stuck in a creative rut and don't know how to get out of it. Often using the same colors over and over leads to a feeling of stagnation. Sometimes something as simple as switching the colors you use will jump-start the creative battery a bit. In the next chapter, we explore the painting process and show a virtually identical painting done in two contrasting color schemes.

# PAINTING A STRANGE-LOOKING CHARACTER

This chapter covers several different concepts, including the creative use of texture—in particular, the use of texture to paint skin and background and the use of different color themes with the same subject. Many times, the skin we paint onto our characters gives the impression of an airbrushed photo. Now, someone wouldn't really mistake a painting of a monster with a photo, but much of the time the simple blemishes, scars, and flaws that make interesting viewing are eliminated or overlooked. The demonstration in this chapter will show you how to go about painting some of these types of skin effects so that you can produce a visually exciting image; it will also expand on these techniques so that you can apply them to backgrounds.

This chapter will also show the use of different color themes on the same subject matter. Why is this important? It is presented as a way to stir an artist's creativity. Often as artists we get into a comfort zone that we resist breaking out of. Sometimes this comfort zone gets boring, and we feel that we are out of ideas or our work is lacking that creative spark. Often it is nothing more than changing something as simple as the colors we are using to break out of the artistic doldrums. This chapter will show the same subject, in this case a face, painted with two very different color schemes. While this is by no means the only way to add a spark of creativity to our work, this is often a good way to start.

Often deciding which colors to use can be problematic. If we are feeling in a rut, the colors we choose may not be different enough from the colors we normally use to give that creative spark. Fortunately, Photoshop offers an easy way to give you some new and very different colors to paint with.

The first part of the chapter will cover how to give yourself different palettes to start painting your new and more creative image. We will then take the same image and, step by step, paint it in different color schemes, finally using custom brushes to add interesting colors to both the skin and background.

This chapter builds on the things you learned in previous chapters, especially in Chapter 15, which is about painting a face. If you have not yet looked at Chapter 15, take a minute to check it out. You should also be familiar with Chapter 17, which examines painting a face using textures, because much of that fundamental information will not be presented again here.

We will be painting a rather strange-looking character so that we can exaggerate the effects and still have the look be appropriate for the subject. As expected, this demonstration is done in Photoshop CS.

## WHAT YOU NEED TO KNOW ABOUT PHOTOSHOP FOR THIS CHAPTER

The following demonstration assumes that you know the following fundamentals of working in Photoshop CS:

- Where individual palettes are located
- How to adjust a brush's opacity
- How to create layers and change their composite method
- How to resize your brush and sample color from within the image (preferably using hot keys)

You can arrange the Photoshop workspace to suit your own liking, so this chapter does not discuss where to locate specific items.

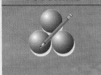

**TUTORIAL**

## GETTING STARTED

The focus of this demonstration is twofold—creating and using a completely different palette than you are used to and, as it was in Chapter 15—painting skin. However, this time, you will learn about other techniques that will allow you to add blemishes and imperfections. While flawless skin is beautiful, it is not that common in the real world. If you can add small imperfections to flawless skin, the believability of your painting, as well as its visual appeal, will be enhanced. For some reason, things that are not pretty and perfect seem to be much more interesting to look at. We hope these techniques will make your images all the more intriguing.

First let's create some new palettes that you can use with your images. One of the more distracting things about digital painting is the sheer number of colors you can choose from. For most artists these days you have the option of choosing any of 16 million colors. That is truly an awesome amount and, quite frankly, way too many. Often as in traditional painting, the premise of using a limited palette will serve you well in digital painting. The question then becomes, how do you limit your palette? Fortunately, this is very simple in Photoshop and depends on the Swatches palette. Figure 18.1 shows Photoshop's Swatches palette with the default 122 colors loaded. This is really quite a drop in the available colors from 16 million, yet this is really too many as well. A good number would be anywhere from 16 to 24 colors.

One of the best ways to get a completely new palette to work with right in Photoshop is to use an image in which you already admire the

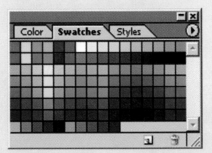

**FIGURE 18.1**  Photoshop's Swatches palette.

color scheme. Figure 18.2 shows an image that we will use to generate new swatches of color to paint with.

In the Image menu, select Mode/Indexed Color. This will bring up the options box shown in Figure 18.3. Within this options box, reduce the

**FIGURE 18.2**    The original image used to create a new Swatches palette.

number of colors to anywhere from 16 to 24. Click the Preview box if you are curious what your image will look like with various reductions in color. It really does not matter what happens to the original image. Play with the different settings, but do not let the number of colors grow to more than 24.

We now have an image that has been reduced to no more than 24 colors, but how do you get those colors into a Swatches palette you can

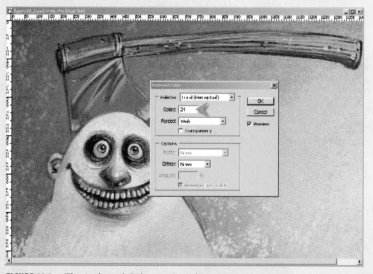

**FIGURE 18.3**    The Indexed Color options box.

use? It is very simple. In the Image menu once again, select Mode/Color Table. Photoshop will display a box that shows the 24 colors that now make up the image (see Figure 18.4). Click the Save button and you will be presented with a box asking you for a name and a folder where you will be saving. Leave the default format as a Color Table, name the Color Table something you can remember, and save it to a location that you will also remember.

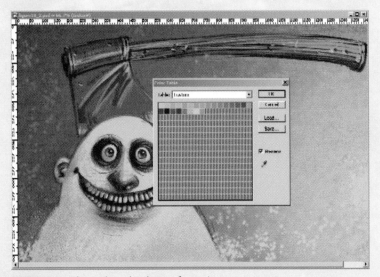

**FIGURE 18.4**    The reduced palette of your image.

From the Swatches menu, select Replace Swatches and select the Color Table you just created. You will now see the colors from your indexed image loaded as your Swatches palette (see Figure 18.5).

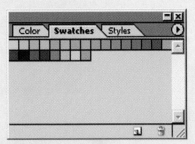

**FIGURE 18.5**    The new Color Table loaded as the Swatches palette.

Now remember, we will ultimately have more than 24 colors in our final painting as we blend and push the color around. This is fine and what we expected. Starting with only up to 24 colors is our goal. To be able to create a pleasing painting with so few colors is entirely possible, as our original painting shows when reduced to 24 colors. You should create a number of different Color Tables that you will be able to load and use, but if you do not want to, a sampling has been provided on the CD-ROM in this chapter's folder.

A number of small shareware programs are available on the Web that will also generate pleasing color palettes for you using different color harmonies.

Now that you have learned how to reduce an image to a minimum number of colors and have created new Swatches palettes from those colors, you are ready to start painting.

The following image is painted in two ways with two different color palettes, one with 16 and the other with 12 colors. The palettes in the top-right corner of the image are for illustration purposes only and represent the colors in the Swatches palette.

When you're ready to start, follow these steps:

1. Start Photoshop as usual. Arrange your palettes to suit your particular working methods.
2. Open the scanned sketch or create a new image that is approximately 1200 (1200 pixels in dimension, and with a resolution between 200 and 300 dpi.) Figure 18.6 shows a scanned drawing. This rather strange-looking fellow is scanned at 300 dpi.

**FIGURE 18.6**    A scanned image.

3. Save your result with the name of your choice, followed by "01." Make it a habit to save numerically named versions of your work. One of the best things about digital painting is this ability to save multiple versions that you can revert to if you make a major mistake.

We are first going to paint the sketch using a cool, analogous color scheme. Analogous colors are those that are located next to each other on the color wheel.

## Painting a Face Using a Cool, Analogous Color Scheme

Select Load Swatches in the Swatches palette and open a cool palette that you have created from another image or by hand. If you would rather use the swatches that were used in the creation of the tutorial image, you can load the swatches from this chapter's folder on the CD-ROM.

*ON THE CD*

The first thing that we need to do is to get rid of all the white in the image and set the base color we want to build the image around. Select, copy, and paste the whole image back into itself. You now have two layers with identical images on each.

Select one of the blue colors from the Swatches palette. It is generally a good idea to start with a color that is located between the ends of the palette instead of one of the colors at the extreme end. This will make achieving a color harmony easier as you paint. When you have selected the color, click on that color in the toolbar. This brings up the color picker. Do not move the small circle to change the color. All you are going to do here is note the RGB, HSV, or LAB values for this particular color. There is no reason to worry about the CMYK values now. Figure 18.7 shows the color picker and where you can find the RGB values for the selected color. Either remember these values or, better yet, write them down on a piece of scrap paper as we will need them in just a moment.

With the background layer active, select Lighting Effects from the Filter/Render menu. In the Lighting Effects options box, click on the Light Type color box. This will take you back to the color picker. Enter the RGB values that you wrote down previously in the RGB boxes here and click OK. Set the Light type to Omni and place this light as shown in Figure 18.8. Adjust the intensity to your liking and click OK.

Your painting should now look something like Figure 18.9. You should have two layers. The top layer's blend mode should be set to Multiply, and this layer will only be visible should you need a guide to reestablish your drawing. For now, hide the top layer.

Create a new layer on top of the background layer. This will be where we do the actual painting of the face. It is generally a good idea to separate the painting of the major pieces of a digital painting onto separate layers. This approach will make changes much easier. Selecting colors

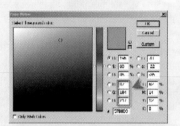

**FIGURE 18.7**    The color picker
with the RGB values highlighted.

**FIGURE 18.8**    The Lighting Effects options box.

from your loaded swatches, begin to block in the colors of the face. Figure
18.10 shows the beginning stages of painting in the character. Do not
worry about details at this point, but try to cover a lot of the image as
quickly as possible. Work from your darkest darks to the lightest lights.
You may have already noticed that all of the colors in this particular
palette are generally the same value. Because this is the case, you will
need to take some of the colors into a darker range and some into a
lighter range as you paint. This is easy to do without changing the Hue
you are using. Simply click on the color to bring up the color picker. We
will be using the HSV buttons to change the brightness of the color.
When the color picker is opened, H will probably be selected. Click B, two
dots below the H. Now you will notice the small vertical bar that had displayed the full spectrum now instead displays the current color in a gradient from very dark to as light as possible for this specific color. Simply
move the sliders up or down this gradient to change the brightness of
your color. This is shown in Figure 18.11.

   This is really a somewhat mechanical way to select color, and you
should feel free to try other methods. The goal is to try to stay as true to
your palette as possible, and a little variation will not matter.

   You will notice that on a new layer, in the upper-right corner of the
image, I have dropped in a small image made from the swatches of the
palette. This is so I can simply use the eyedropper tool to select the colors
and not constantly move to the Swatches palette to change my working
color. This is strictly a personal choice, and you will ultimately find a
method that works best for you.

**FIGURE 18.9**    The two-layer image now looking very blue.

**FIGURE 18.10**    Beginning to paint the skin and hair using the swatches from the color palette.

Continue to paint in the skin using colors selected from your swatches. Notice that we are keeping the brightest colors in the areas where the brightest color would naturally be found in a face. These areas are the cheeks, lips, nose, and ears. Figure 18.12 shows our continued efforts.

**FIGURE 18.11**    The B button selected in the color picker.

**FIGURE 18.12** More work in the face.

**FIGURE 18.13** Additional work on the face.

Now, let's darken the hair more (see Figure 18.13). Using the blending technique described in Chapter 11 at a low opacity, smooth and blend some of the color that you have applied to the face. At this point in our efforts, most of the underlying sketch is covered. If you think you are losing your drawing, unhide the top layer and check things out. Make any adjustments that you feel are necessary and turn the layer off again.

Using a greenish color to contrast  with the brighter purplish colors, paint in a rim light on the shadow side of the character's face, as shown in Figure 18.14.

Create a new layer for the next step. This layer should be above the face layer, and you can name it "sweater" or any other descriptive name. It is always a good idea to name your layers to avoid confusion when you are searching for the correct layer to paint on. This particular image has so few layers that naming it is not critical other than it is a good habit to get into. On this new layer, rough in some sort of clothing or sweater. Once again, detail is not important. Back on the face layer, using a combination of brushes and erasers, clean up the contour of the hair. You don't want to have sharp edges everywhere but a nice mix of sharp and soft. (See Figure 18.15.)

Paint in the iris of the eye using one of your brightest colors, in this case the brightest red you have (Figure 18.16). If you see an area that you feel is getting too rough, go back and blend the colors lightly.

Since this is a rather unusual-looking character, we emphasize that fact by adding some facial decoration (see Figure 18.17). Make it whatever you like: a tattoo, paint, or in this case, a carving. Remember the most important rule: create a new layer before you do anything like this.

**FIGURE 18.14**    Rim light added to the shadow side of the face.

**FIGURE 18.15**    Painting in the clothing on a separate layer, cleaning up the contour of the hair, and putting color into the eye.

If you do not like the decoration, you can always clear the layer and start again without ruining any other part of your painting.

At this point the image is looking pretty good but, quite frankly, somewhat boring. This is probably because the handling of the painting

**FIGURE 18.16**    Painting the iris of the eye with a bright color.

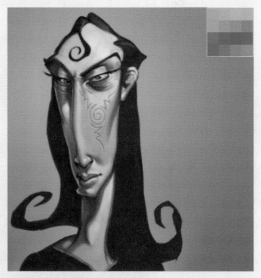

**FIGURE 18.17**    There is nothing like a little face decoration.

has been straightforward, using only one or two brushes combined with blending. The background would also be better if it were not quite so light, so we will darken the background and add some interesting visual texture. Select, copy, and paste the entire background layer back into the image. Change the blend mode of this new layer to Multiply. This is much better as the background has now gotten quite a bit darker and our pale friend's face stands out much better. Adjust the Opacity sliders if you think the background is too light to something that you find pleasing. Remember, there is no one correct look. Figure 18.18 shows the painting with the background layer darkened. I also deleted the layer with the color palette layer as it is really not useful anymore. All color selecting that I need to do is done within the image itself.

ON THE CD

Create a new layer right above the duplicated background layer. Using custom brushes that you have made or ones that are on the CD-ROM, paint in a number of interesting textures, selecting your colors from both the background and the face. Of course, we do not have to worry about any of these textures painting into the face because we are painting on a layer that is underneath the face layer. Figure 18.19 shows the textures painted using colors from within the face. This is particularly evident just to the right of the face, where you can see some of the purples from the cheek area in the background.

The skin is also too flat and lifeless. To add realism to your work and help get away from that look (which screams digital airbrush), add subtle textures into the skin. Load the face texture brushes from this chapter's

**FIGURE 18.18**   The background layer darkened significantly.

**FIGURE 18.19**   Textures painted on their own layer in the background.

folder on the CD-ROM into Photoshop. These brushes were created specifically to add subtle textures into skin in digital paintings. When the brushes are loaded, create a new layer on top of the face layer and paint in subtle textures using colors selected for various areas in the face. Don't worry about some of the paint spilling over onto the hair or darker areas of the skin. This is very easy to correct since we are painting on a new layer. Figure 18.20 shows the textures painted into the skin.

**FIGURE 18.20**    Skin textures painted on their own layer.

If you want to experiment and get more depth, paint multiple textures using differing blend modes one on top of the other.

When you have a number of different and interesting textures painted on the skin, select the Eraser tool and go in and clean up wherever the textures were painted over areas they should not have been. Figure 18.21 shows the face with textures cleaned up.

There are only one or two small steps left before we finish. First, hide the face layer, merge down the background layers into one layer, and define the background as a pattern. Select the whole background, copy, and paste it back into the image. You should now have a layer that is a duplicate of the background. Double-click on this newly created layer to open the Layer Style options. Check the Bevel and Emboss box. Duplicate the settings you see in Figure 18.22, 18.23, and 18.24. In Figure 18.23 note the Contour setting in particular. If you do not have this option set this way, you will have a bevel around your whole image. In Figure 18.24, the pattern to use is the one you defined from the background.

**FIGURE 18.21** The facial textures cleaned up.

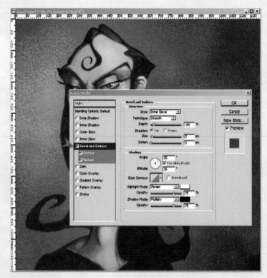

**FIGURE 18.22** The Bevel and Emboss options in the Layer Style menu.

**FIGURE 18.23** The Contour options in the Layer Style/Bevel and Emboss options.

**FIGURE 18.24** The Texture options in the Layer Style/Bevel and Emboss options.

And the last thing to do is this: the carving on the face is just too big. Select the layer where this decoration is located and under the Edit menu, choose Transform and Scale. Size the decoration to whatever size suits you. The image is finally finished. Figure 18.25 shows the final image painted with a cool color scheme and one that we would not have chosen in the regular course of our painting.

**FIGURE 18.25**    The finished image.

## Painting a Face Using a Warm Color Scheme

ON THE CD

In this section, we are going to switch gears completely and head in a direction that is 180 degrees from the previous image. Again, we will be using swatches either culled from an existing image or handmade. The Swatches palette used is on the CD-ROM if you care to use it. This image, though of the same subject matter, will have a completely different feel from the previous one solely because of the colors we are using. Again, this is a marvelous way to spark creativity if you have hit a slump.

Because most of the techniques used are virtually identical to the previous image, only cursory instructions will be given with each image. Where something new is used, a more in-depth explanation will be given.

So let's start. Open the sketch you started with in the previous section and make sure that the colors you will limit yourself to are loaded into the Swatches palette. Copy and paste the entire image back into itself, change the new layers' blend mode to Multiply, and hide the layer.

Using the same technique described previously, render a lighting effect using one of the colors from the swatches to get rid of all the white in the image. (See Figure 18.26.)

**FIGURE 18.26**    The two-layer image with a warm lighting effect applied.

On a new layer, block in the major colors of the face (Figure 18.27). Remember this can be rough at this stage as you are only trying to establish the color scheme.

On the same layer, continue to refine, darken, and blend the colors where needed. Keep the brightest colors where appropriate (Figure 18.28).

Add a rim light to the shadow side of the face (Figure 18.29). Pick a color that is complementary to the brighter colors for interest.

Create a new layer and on this layer, rough in some clothing. Back on the face layer, using a combination of brushes and erasers, clean up the contour of the hair. Paint in the iris of the eye using one of your brightest and most contrasting colors. (See Figure 18.30.)

We are not going to carve anything into this character, but it would be nice to have some decoration, so let's add some jewelry. Create a new layer and paint the stud in the corner of the nose. To duplicate this for the additional three studs, you could select the stud using the lasso tool and copy and paste it. While this is a perfectly fine solution to the problem, you will end up with a lot of layers to deal with, so let's use a different approach since we are not painting a too complicated image. Select the stud with the lasso tool but instead of using copy and paste, hold down the Ctrl and Alt keys (PC) and drag a copy of your selection above the first stud. Continue this until you have the number you would like duplicated. No-

**FIGURE 18.27**    The block-in of the major colors of the face.

**FIGURE 18.28**    Some blending, darkening, and refining of the painting.

**FIGURE 18.29**    Adding the rim light.

**FIGURE 18.30**    Adding clothing on a new layer, cleaning up the hair, and painting the iris.

tice that one was also put up by the eyebrow. The nice thing about this technique is that all of your duplicates are on the same layer. Just make sure you know where you are placing them or you will have to go back in and individually select each one to move. Paint any remaining jewelry you may want on this layer or an additional one. (See Figure 18.31.)

This background would also be better if it were not quite as light. Let's darken the background and add some interesting visual texture. Select, copy, and paste the background layer back into the image. Change the blend mode of this new layer to Multiply. This is much better as the background is again now quite a bit darker but, in this case, way too warm for the face. In the Image/Adjustments/Hue and Saturation options, take the saturation of the layer down until it is almost gray. As this layer interacts with the background, the color temperature is much more pleasing. Adjust the Opacity sliders if you think the background is too dark to something that you find pleasing. Create a new layer and on this layer add all the textural elements using custom brushes that you have built or the ones located on the CD-ROM. Figure 18.32 shows the image with a darker background and textures added. When you have finished adding the textures, merge all the background layers down.

**FIGURE 18.31** Jewelry and studs added.

**FIGURE 18.32** The darker, textured background.

The face in this image also needs some texture added to make it more visually interesting. Using the technique described above, add texture to the skin. Figure 18.33 shows a closeup of the face with textures added.

Our final task is to add some depth to the textures in the background layer. Do this as described in detail earlier. To simplify, define a pattern from the entire background layer and, using layer styles, add some beveling and embossing using your newly defined pattern. Figure 18.34 shows the finished image.

Hopefully in this chapter you have learned several very important things. First, we showed you a way to spark your creativity when you feel

**FIGURE 18.33**    Textures added to the skin of the figure.

that you have lost that edge by using different and unusual color schemes that you have created from scratch or works of art that inspire you. Second, you saw how to use texture to enliven a painting not only in the background but in something we normally would think of as smooth: skin. 🍒

**FIGURE 18.34**    The finished image.

## CONCLUSION

In this chapter, we painted a character with a less-than-perfect complexion in two different color schemes using Photoshop's swatches. Almost always, adding some flaws and imperfections will make your paintings much more visually interesting. What you learned here is only a small portion of the possibilities we hope you will explore within your own work. In the next chapter, we will paint a character with a candle as a light source.

# PAINTING A CREATURE AND A CANDLE

This chapter, which builds on techniques learned in previous chapters, covers two major themes: painting a rather strange blue creature, and painting a candle as a light source. You will create custom brushes for both subjects and explore their usage. All of the patterns and brushes are included on the CD-ROM for your convenience. It is hoped, however, that you will learn how to create these types of patterns and brushes on your own to expand your range of creative possibilities.

As usual, the tutorial is done in Photoshop CS. While many of the Photoshop techniques might work with other applications, their implementation may or may not be far more difficult, and some of the techniques described in this chapter, such as layer styles, really have no counterpart in other applications.

## WHAT YOU NEED TO KNOW ABOUT PHOTOSHOP FOR THIS CHAPTER

This tutorial assumes that you know some fundamentals of working in Photoshop, such as:

- Where individual palettes are located
- How to adjust a brush's opacity
- How to create and save a pattern
- How to create layers and change their blend mode
- How to resize your brush and sample color from within the image (preferably using the hot keys)
- How to create a layer style
- How to create brushes

You can arrange the Photoshop workspace to suit your own liking, so this chapter does not discuss where to locate specific items.

## TUTORIAL    PAINTING A RATHER DOUR-LOOKING BLUE CHARACTER STANDING BY A CANDLE

The focus of this tutorial is the character with reflected light and the candle with its glowing light. Both these subjects can be frustrating to the artist because of their seeming complexity. Though they seem complex, the digital world makes them much easier to paint than doing so ever was in the traditional world. The secrets of painting these subjects effectively are to simplify and to let the application do most of the work.

### Getting Started

To begin painting your blue character, follow these steps:

1. Start Photoshop as usual. Open your scanned sketch, or create a new image that is approximately 1800 pixels in height. Figure 19.1 shows

a grouchy but generally likable creature. He has been scanned at 200 dpi in grayscale because we don't want to carry over to the finished painting any of the color or texture from the drawing paper. As you can see, the sketch is far from complete, yet we're not too concerned about this because we want to further develop the idea in the sketch. Do not spend hours drawing an extremely detailed sketch because you will only overpaint it. Your goal is to work smarter and not necessarily harder. The sketch is located on the CD-ROM for you to use if you do not have one of your own or if you do not have a scanner to scan one of your sketches.

ON THE CD

**FIGURE 19.1**    The scanned sketch.

2. Once in Photoshop, resize the image so that it is no larger than 1800 pixels in the largest dimension. We really do not need an image that is larger in the beginning stages of a painting as we are not concerned with small areas in the painting at this point. We will increase the size of the image as we get to the point where we are adding more detail. Always save numerically named versions of your work so you can recover your work if you make a major mistake.

3. At this point in the painting process, you need to decide what mood you want to convey in the image as well as what the main colors of the character and the environment will be. It's a good idea to do a number of color comps. These are very small images painted quickly to get a feel of the color scheme that you are looking for. They should take no longer than five to ten minutes each. Traditionally, these comps could be time consuming, but digitally there is no excuse for not doing at least one or two. Figure 19.2 shows an example of a color comp. In it, we have decided to make the main character a bluish color, and the environment slightly darker and complementary. The darker complementary environment will directly contrast the color of the main character and (we hope) will give some interest to the composition. Do not be afraid of making a wrong decision about the colors and environment; you can change them later. At this point, sometimes the hardest part of a painting is starting. Making a few preliminary decisions will at least get you working.

**FIGURE 19.2** Color comp.

4. Now is a good time to decide what you are going to use as your main painting tool. This decision, though not a fundamental decision for the outcome of a successful image, most likely will affect several other steps in the painting process. For most of the painting in our blue character image, we will be using the Airbrush Pen Opacity Flow in various sizes and opacities; this is one of Photoshop's default brushes. If you cannot see this brush in the Brush Preset Picker, reset your brushes. This brush is a good general-purpose brush that is easy to control when building up color.

## Removing the White Areas in the Image

After you have made your color comp and thought about what you will do, it's time to get rid of the white areas in the image. Doing this is easy, and there are a number of simple techniques to accomplish this. This section discusses commonly used ways.

Before we get into how to remove the white, you need to start by copying and pasting the image of your character into a new layer. Double-click on the layer and name it Sketch or something similar. Go ahead and hide the layer you have just created so it is not visible at this time. Create a new layer, drag it under the layer with your creature's sketch, and fill the layer with color of your choice using either the Paint Bucket Tool alone or by rendering a lighting effect using Filter/Render/Lighting Effects over a colored fill. The Lighting Effects filter will not work on a transparent layer. We have decided to use the Lighting Effects and fill an already filled layer with a greenish-tan combination of colors. These colors will be a good complementary base for the main character. The layer is filled with an opaque combination of tan and greenish colors. Make sure that this new layer is active. Now here are your three choices (or you can do a combination of them) for removing the white areas of the picture:

- Reduce the opacity of the layer to something less than 100%.
- Under the Edit menu, select the Fade command and apply this at whatever percentage looks good to you. You will use the Fade command a lot with almost all filter operations.
- Change the blend mode of the layer to Multiply. This not only makes the layer transparent but somewhat increases the contrast as a whole for the image.

We have decided to set the layer's Mode to Multiply. The results, shown in Figure 19.3, leave us with a brownish image to work with. Merge down the layer on to your background, and save your image.

**FIGURE 19.3**   Setting the Mode to Multiply.

## Painting the Blue Character

Now it's time to paint our sullen friend. Follow these steps:

1. Make the layer with your character's sketch visible and change its blend mode to Multiply. This causes all the white of the layer to become transparent and lets you see the original sketch over the background layer. This will become useful in later steps to check the accuracy of your drawing as you paint over the background. Create a new layer and, with one of the Airbrush Soft Round brushes, begin to block in the color for the character. This should be done on the layer that is between the background and sketch layer. Your strokes will begin to cover the sketch but never mind; this is why we have the top sketch layer set to Multiply. Do not try to stay within the lines. It is more important to work quickly and establish the general color theme and clean up the ledges later. Figure 19.4 shows the layer being painted with the Airbrush. Notice how it is indeed covering the sketch underneath.

**FIGURE 19.4**    Airbrushing color onto a new layer over the background sketch.

2. Using the Eraser tool, clean up the edges of the color that we have airbrushed on the middle layer. Make the Sketch layer visible to give you a guide if your airbrush strokes have covered your underlying sketch. Figure 19.5 shows the middle layer with the edges cleaned up and the top Sketch layer visible as a guide.

3. Our little blue fellow is centrally located within the canvas. This is not good as we are going to want to add a candle in front of him. We need more canvas to work with. In the Image menu, select Canvas Size. Click the middle box that is highlighted by the red arrow. This will increase the size of the canvas to the left of our character, giving us the room needed to add a candle. In the Width box, increase the size to 1800 pixels. This gives us a square image. Figure 19.6 shows the Canvas Size box with the new settings.

4. As you can now see, our character is not located off center to the right of the image. There is now enough space to eventually add a candle. However, you will note a distinct problem with the image at this point. There is a white band on the left side of the canvas. It may be another color, depending on what your background color was set to.

**FIGURE 19.5**    The results of using the Eraser tool to clean up the edges of the character.

**FIGURE 19.6**    The Canvas Size box.

Quite obviously, we need to get rid of this. We have several ways to do this. One would be to fill the area on the canvas with a custom gradient, but we are going to use another approach. Select all the background, copy it, and paste it back into the image. With the Magic Wand tool, select the white area and hit the Delete or Backspace key. This gets rid of the white but you now have transparent over the background layer. Open the first saved version of this painting where you first finished creating the background. Copy the background from this image and paste it into your current image. Move this layer below the image with the character on it, and move the bottom layer around until it fills the transparent area. Then merge these two layers. You may need to move around your airbrush color layer and the top sketch layer to get them into alignment. Figure 19.7 shows the result of all this layer copying and pasting.

**FIGURE 19.7**    The larger image with the background cut and pasted.

5. Using the blending technique described in Chapter 11, we blend the edges together the best we can. We also decide that our character needs a floor to stand on. Up to this point he has been floating in the air. Possibly a checkered floor would be a nice touch. Using Photoshop's guides, set up a grid in the image that creates a nice checkerboard pattern. The exact sizes of each grid space will be determined by the image size. When the grid is set up, make sure that the Snap to Grid option is checked, then use the rectangular selection and make a selection of one of the grid sections. Hold down the Shift key and continue to make rectangular selections, forming a checkerboard pattern. Save your selection. On the new layer, using any brush of your choice, paint in the dark or light tiles. Invert the selection and paint in the opposite color tiles. Save your file. You now have an image where the character is on one layer, the checkerboard floor is on another layer, and the sketch is still on the topmost layer. Figure 19.8 shows the image to this point.

6. When painting both traditionally and digitally, it is a good idea to set the value range of your painting early. Begin painting with darker colors but indicate where some of your lightest lights will be located.

**FIGURE 19.8**   Blending the background and painting in the checkered floor.

Block in color in both the figure and the background. Do not get into the coloring-book habit of trying to stay in the lines, but do get in the habit of saving your image as you progress. The image to this point is a good example of this.

7. Notice in the previous image that the character is crooked on the floor. We need to straighten him up a bit to be sitting more vertically. This step also takes a bit of courage on the artist's part as we are going to merge the character's colored and sketch layers. Hide the background and floor layers. Make sure that one of the remaining visible layers is active and select the Merge Visible command. The colored and sketch layers are combined into one. We have one problem: there is now a white box around the character. Select the white color using the Magic Wand tool and press Backspace or Delete. Unhide the two other layers and have a look. There is a rough white halo around the character. Never fear, as we work we will clean this edge up using a combination of brush tools and the Eraser tool. From the Edit menu, select Transform/Rotate and rotate your character until he is more vertical and flat on the floor. Figure 19.9 shows the character in a more level stance.

**FIGURE 19.9**    The characters layers are merged and then rotated to a more vertical position.

8. Begin to reestablish the drawing of the character, working from the darker colors to the lighter. Using the Eraser tool, erase some of the white from the edges. Make sure you are working on the character's layer and not on the background or the checkered floor layer. Save your image at this point (see Figure 19.10).

**FIGURE 19.10**  Establishing some of the darks and erasing some of the white edges.

9. The character is low on the floor, so we move the layer up until the character is sitting on the top of the checkered floor. As you can see in Figure 19.11, the form is starting to develop and feel more substantial and the color is rich. We have begun to work on some of the smaller details, such as the eyes and nose.

10. We continue to do a significant amount of work on the character. His general color from the tip of the ears to the feet is mostly established at this point. Additional work is done in the smaller detail areas such as the eyes, nose, and ears. Figure 19.12 shows our character at this point.

11. Figure 19.13 shows a closeup of the character's face to reveal the level of detail and finish at this point.

**FIGURE 19.11**    Moving the character up to sit on the top of the floor and working on some of the smaller details.

**FIGURE 19.12**    The character with richer color and additional work in the detail areas.

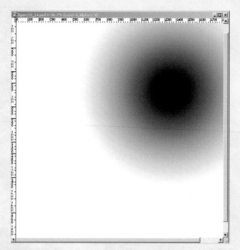

**FIGURE 19.14**  The new alpha channel.

**FIGURE 19.13**  A closeup of the face showing the level of detail at this point in the painting process.

12. Now is a good time to begin thinking about how to handle the background surrounding the character. Right now the background is way too light to paint in a candle and have it look like it is glowing with light, so we need to darken it in some way. We do not want an overall dark feeling, though, and would like to keep a bit of light background against the dark side of the character. Here is a way to do this. Create a new alpha channel and fill it with a radial gradient. The channel should look something like Figure 19.14.

13. Make sure the background layer is active. Load the alpha channel you just created as a selection. Copy the background using the selection and paste it back into the image. Change the blend mode for the new layer to Multiply. Figure 19.15 shows the new layer at this point. Notice how much darker the background layer looks. You may want to change the opacity of the new background layer slightly to suit your taste.

14. The color of the background needs to be changed to be more in harmony with the character. Make sure that the new background layer is active and in the Image menu, select Adjustments/Hue and Saturation. Move the Hue slider around until you establish a pleasing color theme. Merge this layer with the background (see Figure 19.16).

**FIGURE 19.15**    The second background layer with its blend mode set to Multiply.

15. At this point you cannot really tell where the figure is in the space of the painting. Now is the time to add a shadow of the creature on the back wall to give a sense of space in the image. The position of the shadow can give a visual clue as to how deep the space is in the picture. In this particular case, we want the picture space to be relatively shallow, so the shadow will be higher in the picture plane. To create the shadow, do the following. Make sure that the layer with the character is the active layer. Hold down the Ctrl key and click on the layer with the stylus or mouse. Everything that is not transparent is automatically selected, which is exactly what we want. You will notice there is a line of "marching ants" around the character. Create a new layer and name it Shadow. With your selection still active, fill the selection on the new layer with a dark color selected with the eyedropper tool from somewhere in the background. Clear the selection so that nothing is selected. From the Filter menu, select Blur/Gaussian Blur. In the preview window that is now displayed, move the slider to get a nice blur. For an image this size, a radius of

**FIGURE 19.16**    The color theme of the image is more cohesive and harmonious.

about 20 pixels will give a nice effect. Figure 19.17 shows the image and Gaussian Blur preview window.

16. Our shadow layer is on top of the character layer. Click and hold on the Shadow layer and drag it down below the floor layer. The only layer that should be behind the Shadow layer is the background. With the Move tool, move the Shadow layer to the left and down from the figure. Change the blend mode to Multiply and adjust the opacity to suit your tastes. Figure 19.18 shows the Shadow layer moved into place. It now appears that the main light on the character is coming from the top right and casting the creature's shadow on the wall behind him. Once again, save your file.

17. It is time to add the candle to the painting. We will put it sitting on the checkered floor just to the left of the creature. It will be created on two separate layers. One layer will be for the flame and one layer for the candle itself. Create a new layer and paint in the candle body. It is a very good idea to have a good photographic reference or an actual candle burning in front of you. Notice how the flame makes the somewhat translucent candle slightly lighter nearer the flame. Take into consideration the prevailing direction of the main light and paint the body of the candle accordingly. Use the same brush but with

**FIGURE 19.17**    Gaussian Blur applied to the shadow layer.

**FIGURE 19.18**    The creature now has a shadow on the wall behind him.

slightly less opacity so that the colors can be built up gradually. Paint in the candlewick with a slight glow at its tip. Figure 19.19 shows the painted candle.

18. On a new layer, paint the candle flame. Pay special attention to all the subtle colors visible (see Figure 19.20).

19. If you are not happy with the position of the candle, link the layers and move both layers together until you find a position within the painting that you like. Figure 19.21 shows the final position of the candle in the painting. Notice how the candle is positioned in a very dark area of the background. This is not by accident since the best way to make something look light is to place it next to something dark. We want the candle to look very light.

**FIGURE 19.19**   The painted candle.

**FIGURE 19.20**   The painted candle flame.

20. Create an additional layer to paint the subtle glow around the candle flame. We will be changing the blend mode of this layer to Vivid Light. You may want to work on the layer in the Normal mode or in the Vivid Light mode. Using one of the larger airbrush tools at a low opacity and starting with a red color, gradually replacing it with a yellow, paint in the glow around the candle flame. Figure 19.22 shows a closeup of the painted candle glow. When you have results that you like, save the image once again. It may seem redundant to keep saving the image but losing an hour's or more work can be very painful.

21. Figure 19.23 shows the whole image and how the glow interacts with the background.

22. Let's begin to paint in the background and get something more interesting happening than a simple gradient. Load the brushes in the Chapter 19 folder on the CD-ROM. These brushes were used to give

ON THE CD

**FIGURE 19.21**   The painted candle in relationship to the creature in the painting.

the background the varied and rough texture. Using the brushes in larger sizes (anything around 200 pixels or so should work fine), select a color from the background layer and paint some interesting-looking textures. You can do this on a new layer or directly on the background. If you decide to work the textures on a new layer, make sure that you merge it down to the background when you get a look you like. This is important for the next step in our painting. Since you are working on individual layers, you don't even need to worry about the character. You will also notice that the textures look very nice when painted under the Shadow layer (see Figure 19.24).

23. The textures that we have just created are interesting to look at but slightly flat. They would look better with some feeling of dimension. There is a very easy way to do this in Photoshop and that is using Layer Styles. To create a Layer Style, you simply double-click on the layer you want to apply a style to. It will bring up the Layer Style menu showing numerous check boxes and options. Before we actually get to apply a

**FIGURE 19.22**    The painted candle glow.

**FIGURE 19.23**    The complete painting after painting in the candle glow.

**FIGURE 19.24**    Textures painted into the background to give more interest.

style there is one thing we need to do. In your image, hide all the layers except the background layer. Simply click on the small eye icon to hide the layer. With only the background now visible, go to the Edit menu and select Define Pattern. This will create a new pattern that is identical to your background. Select the background layer and copy and paste it as a new layer. Layer Styles will only work on layers, after all. Double-click the new layer that is a duplicate of your background. The Layer Styles menu appears. We are only going to be concerned with the Bevel and Emboss options, so make sure that menu is checked. Deselect any other options. Two submenus are available: Contour and Texture. Right now we are concerned with the Bevel and Emboss menu. We want to change the default light angle and Highlight Mode color. Figure 19.25 shows the light angle set to 49 degrees and the Highlight Mode color set to something a bit more harmonious with the background than white. You can leave everything else at the default unless you just want to experiment.

24. Highlight the Contour menu. Notice that we have a bevel around the outside of our painting. We want to get rid of this. The shape of this contour is determined by the shape of the small, gray thumbnail. The default is from the lower-left corner to the upper-right corner. We are going to change this. Click on the thumbnail itself and not the small triangle flyout menu. This will bring up the Coutour Editor. Drag the small square all the way to the left side of the displayed graph. Notice how the bevel around the painting disappears. This is the effect we want. Figure 19.26 shows the Contour Editor menu and the position you should move the small square to.

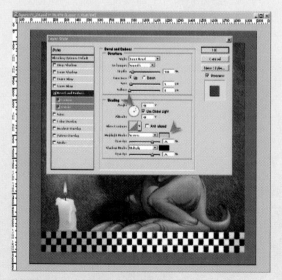

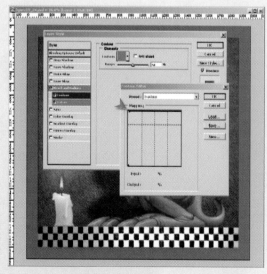

**FIGURE 19.25**   The Bevel and Emboss menu.

**FIGURE 19.26**   The Contour Editor.

25. Highlight the Texture menu under Bevel and Emboss. In the Pattern thumbnail display select the pattern that you created from the background. Do not change the Scale slider but adjust the Depth slider to your own liking. Figure 19.27 shows the Texture menu.

**FIGURE 19.27**    The Texture menu.

26. You will now see a great three-dimensional effect added to your painting's background (see Figure 19.28).

27. More work now needs to be done on the checkered floor. The small checkers are just too busy for the composition, so we will make them larger. Using the same procedure as earlier in the chapter we create a new checkered floor with slightly larger tiles. Because we want it to also appear to interact with the light in the picture, a slight linear gradient is applied over the checks on a new layer, and this gradient layer's blend mode is set to Multiply. Merge these two layers into one and apply a Layer Style as described earlier to give the floor some texture. You do not need to first create a pattern of the checkered floor this time, though. Just pick a nice pattern that will give you a slightly rough look. Figure 19.29 shows the new floor with the Layer Style texture.

28. The floor is still a bit uneven. There is sometimes no better way to fix something than to simply go in and do some painting. With the Airbrush Pen Opacity Flow brush, go in and paint each check to clean up and finish the floor. At this point the creature himself is way too saturated in color for the muted feeling of the rest of the painting. Select the character's layer and adjust down the saturation so he is not quite

**FIGURE 19.28**   The painting with a three-dimensional background.

**FIGURE 19.29**   Changing the checkered floor.

so bright. Figure 19.30 shows the painting at this stage with the checkered floor cleaned up and the saturation of the character adjusted down to make him slightly less colorful.

**FIGURE 19.30**   The adjusted character and reworked floor.

29. Something is just not quite right with the painting. What is missing is the light of the candle shining on the creature. This is the time to add light shining from the candle on the character. Again, to avoid any costly mistakes, create a new layer to do the painting on. Pick an orange color, and begin to paint along the contour of your character. The goal is to get the character looking as if he is being subtly lit from the candle on the floor. As you move along the contours of the character, change the color to a more red color as you get further from the candle flame. As you get closer to the flame, select a slightly more yellow color. Do not make any of these candle colors lighter than the lightest colors on the creature's light side. If you do, you will punch "visual holes" within your painting. When you have reached a point where you are happy with the effect, go ahead and merge these layers. Figure 19.31 shows the light of the candle painted onto the character.

30. The floor still needs a bit of additional work. On a new layer, paint by hand some cracks and holes. You need to paint both the dark crack and the light edge where the crack reflects the light. Doing this will give the illusion of depth. Figure 19.32 shows the painted cracks in the floor.

**FIGURE 19.31**    The candlelight painted onto the character.

**FIGURE 19.32**    Some new cracks in the floor.

31. We are almost finished. He needs a bit of hair on the top of his head. Once again, create a new layer and paint the hair. If you do not like the look of what you paint, simply delete the layer or select the whole layer and delete its contents and try again. We give him a kind of balding little lock of hair. Figure 19.33 shows the new hairpiece on our creature.

**FIGURE 19.33**    Painting in the hairpiece.

32. Now for the final touch. What creature would be complete without some bumpy skin? Painting on a new layer and selecting colors from within the figure itself, paint some bumps on some of the skin areas. They do not have to be perfect as we are looking for a general impression instead of photographic rendering. The image is now finished as shown in Figure 19.34. 🪕

**FIGURE 19.34**    The finished painting.

## Conclusion

In this chapter, we saw that painting two seemingly complicated subjects, a rather strange creature and candlelight, is not as hard as you may have thought. If you use a little planning and forethought, painting this subject matter is no harder than painting anything else. Because you will not only be painting characters that are unclothed, in the next chapter, we will be painting fabric and, more specifically, a white gown on a figure. Chapter 20 focuses on a very basic technique for painting one kind of cloth. Most all other types of fabric, clothing, and costume can be based on these techniques.

# CHAPTER

# 20

# PAINTING THE FABRIC OF A CHARACTER'S COSTUME

U nless you intend to paint your characters nude, there is good reason to learn to paint fabric. It's possible to write an entire book about painting different types of fabric and costume, so this chapter will just describe a basic method for painting fabric.

The two most important things to remember when drawing and painting fabric are:

**Draw and paint the fabric with straight lines.** The thinner the fabric, the straighter and crisper the lines will be. Though fabric often forms beautiful curving lines when draped, if you draw the fabric that way, the drawing will become soft as you work the image, and the fabric will lose much of its form.

**Draw and paint only the major folds that help to describe the form underneath.** There is a distinct difference between folds and wrinkles. Folds originate from points of tension on the figure and help to generally describe the form underneath. Wrinkles are just creases in the fabric.

Another thing to keep in mind is that the material a fold is made of determines the fold's visual weight. For instance, gauze will fall into folds that are very different from leather.

Several different types of folds each have a distinctive look, including these:

- Folds caused by the action of gravity, which causes the fabric to fall on itself
- Folds that originate from objects that are under the fabric
- Folds caused by the wind

This chapter won't be covering kinds of folds. If you want to learn more about them, consult one of the good books out there that describe how folds work.

## WHAT YOU NEED TO KNOW ABOUT PHOTOSHOP FOR THIS CHAPTER

This tutorial assumes that you know some fundamentals of working in Photoshop CS. You should know such things as:

- Where individual palettes are located
- How to create and work with layers
- How to adjust a brush's opacity
- How to resize your brush and sample color from within the image (preferably using hot keys)

*This chapter builds on the things learned in the previous chapters, so we will not repeat the basic information presented there.*

| TUTORIAL | PAINTING FABRIC |

Let's start painting some fabric. Follow these steps:

1. Open Photoshop and create a new image file. If you do not have an image that you want to work with, the sketch that this tutorial used is located on the CD-ROM and can be used. The original image for this painting was created approximately 1584 pixels wide (2100 pixels high), and a photograph was used as a reference. You could scan the image, bring it into your program, and paint over the scanned photo, but you will learn more about the process if you paint over a drawing instead. Do whatever works best for you.

2. The whole image is done with only a few different brushes, with the opacity set at various densities and the size increased and decreased as needed.

3. We will take extra time to establish the face of the character before we draw the costume. This is not the best way to work and is not recommended. However, since this demonstration is about painting the costume, it is appropriate to get the major work on the face done first. Either draw an image similar to the sketch or open the sketch supplied. Figure 20.1 shows the sketch from a reference photo. Notice that at this point not a lot of detail is drawn into the sketch. This is on purpose to help us resist the impulse to just fill in the lines in a coloring-book style.

4. Apply a lighting effect from the Filter menu to get rid of all of the very bright white in the image. A greenish effect is applied to the top of the image and a slightly red effect is placed on the lower half of the image. We chose this lighting scheme for Figure 20.2 because we'd already decided to paint the hair a reddish blonde color and keep the fabric slightly warmer compared to the background. A green and red color scheme is very easy to handle as far as how the colors interact. The lighting is applied to get rid of the white surface of the canvas and to add subtle color that will be used in the actual fabric painting. Save your file.

5. Because this tutorial is about painting fabric, not much time will be spent on describing the process of painting the face, hands, and sword. There is, however, value in showing the procedure as a review on how to handle these subjects. Figure 20.3 shows the face of

**FIGURE 20.1**    The sketch from a reference photo.

the character blocked in on a new layer. Notice that the sketch is not completely covered and we are not trying to "stay within the lines" of the sketch. Painting on a newly created layer makes changes and corrections so very easy.

**FIGURE 20.2**  The sketch with a lighting effect applied.

6. Continuing on the same layer, the hair is finished a bit more and the hand and sword are blocked in. At this stage of the painting (see Figure 20.4), enough finish needs to be done to give a good idea of what the final image will look like, but it would be unwise to try and finish

**FIGURE 20.3**    The face of the girl blocked in on a new layer.

the face and hands at this early stage. Invariably, as we finished the rest of the painting, we would find we needed to go back and repaint sections, if not the entire face. Leaving the face at a more unfinished stage will make it easier to make changes as the painting is completed.

**FIGURE 20.4**    More painting in the blonde hair and blocking in the major values in the hand and sword.

7. Figure 20.5 shows the painting to this point with the face, hands, and part of the sword blocked in. The painting is now ready for us to begin painting the fabric costume. In this case we will actually be painting two separate parts of the costume, the dress and the cape.

8. Create a new layer for the fabric and arrange it so that it is located underneath the layer with the face on it. As when painting with tradi-

**FIGURE 20.5**    The image ready to have the fabric painted.

tional tools, start by laying in the darks first, as shown in Figure 20.6. The first goal is always to establish a strong value statement. In this painting we have tried two different methods of laying in the broad dark shapes. On the right of the image, the brush we have been painting with is used. On the left, one of the default Photoshop airbrushes

**FIGURE 20.6**   The lights and darks of the image blocked in.

is used. The specific brush is Airbrush Soft Round 200. Notice that really no effort is made to stay within the forms. All that we are doing at this point is to try and separate the lights and darks of the costume.

9. Select a dark yellow color and continue to fill in some of the darker areas of the cape (Figure 20.7).

**FIGURE 20.7**    The dark yellows of the cape are also painted in.

10. When the darks are blocked in, we go back into them with a slightly lighter brush and reestablish the directional folds. It is critical that when we are doing this, the color that we are using is dark enough to not punch visual holes into the darks. Try squinting your eyes at the image and see how the lighter colors merge into one large dark shape. Figure 20.8 shows the beginning of this phase as we draw in the folds of the gown.

**FIGURE 20.8** Drawing in the folds of the gown.

11. Once the direction of the folds is established, it is time to start to bring in some of the lighter values in the costume. The right side of the painting shows some of these lighter values being painted in. To maintain interesting contrasts, be sure to keep these lighter values lighter than the background. Also notice that we are not using a pure white but a white that has a distinctly yellowish cast. Figure 20.9 shows the beginning of this process that will spread across the costume.

**FIGURE 20.9**    Painting in some of the lighter values of the costume.

12. An important thing we need to remember when painting white fabric is this: rarely is white fabric white. This may sound like an oxymoron, but it is in fact the truth. When you are painting white costumes, it is important to vary the colors within the fabric slightly instead of using gray values. If you paint white fabric in shades of neutral gray, your painting will lack life and most likely your carefully painted white costume will look gray. In the case of this particular dress, it will pick up some of the color of both the background and the yellow cape. You will notice in the highlighted areas in Figure 20.10 some rather intense and definitely not gray colors painted in to add variety and life to the white costume. Much of the color that is used to paint is sampled from within the image at this stage. It is also a good thing to put these more intense colors on the transition edges from the darks to the lights. If you paint too bright a color into either the light or dark areas, you will change the perceived color of the fabric or make it look like it had dirt or stains on it.

**FIGURE 20.10**    Examples of intense colors added to the white fabric.

13. As you paint you will want to remember that the lightest lights in the fabric are closest to the center of interest, which is the face. As the fabric gets farther and farther away from the head, the values get darker. Because the major patterns that were first sketched were somewhat lost in the initial lay-in, they are reestablished and cleaned up here. Most times when painting fabric, all you will need to do is a convincing job of three values: a dark value for the shadows, a mid-

value for the majority of the fabric, and a light value for the highlights. In this particular painting, the mid-value is more part of the dark shadow than a true mid-tone. Remember that everything is relative and that the mid-value for a white costume is not the same as the mid-value for a darker fabric. As shown in Figure 20.11, the folds

**FIGURE 20.11**    Refining the costume and keeping the lightest lights close to the face, which is the center of interest.

are refined even further; use straight lines and draw with the darkest of the three values. Notice that many of the darker colors in the cape are repeated in the darks of the costume. This is a technique that will help unify your paintings.

14. At this point, the darks of the painting appear too dark and much too muddy. To rectify this, we will use one of the new and quite useful features in Photoshop CS. Make sure that the costume layer is the active layer. In the Adjustments menu go down and select Shadow/Highlight, as shown in Figure 20.12.

**FIGURE 20.12** The Adjustments/Shadow/Highlight menu.

15. You will notice an immediate change in that the shadows of the fabric are lighter and more colorful. For our purposes, the default setting seems to have handled making the shadows less heavy and dreary-looking (see Figure 20.13), but feel free to play around with the sliders until you get a look that you like.

16. Continue to define and refine the folds of the costume into the shadow area of the figure, as shown in Figure 20.14. Figure 20.15 shows a closer look at the continuation of this process in the lower part of the figure. Notice the variety of colors used in the shadows. Figure 20.16 shows the whole painting to this stage.

17. Now it is time to start working on the cape part of the costume. Working in much the same way as you did in earlier stages of the image, select some golden colors, and working from dark to light, rough in the cape as in Figure 20.17. This can be done on a separate layer or, in this case, on the same layer as the white gown.

**FIGURE 20.13**     The results of using the Shadow/Highlight adjustment.

18. The costume is beginning to look pretty good at this point, but the image overall is looking fairly boring. A simple way to fix this would be to add some interest into the very plain background. Because we

**FIGURE 20.14**    A continued refining of the fabric on the shadow side of the costume.

have painted both the face and the costume on separate layers, adding interest to the background is an easy chore. Individual layers will eliminate the necessity of carefully painting around the contour

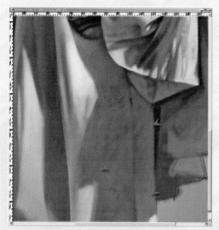

**FIGURE 20.15**  Notice the variety of colors used in the shadows of the closeup of the costume.

**FIGURE 20.16**  The whole painting to this point.

*ON THE CD*

of the figure if all the work had been done on one layer. Figure 20.18 shows a texture selected to use for a background because of its sky-like feel. This texture file can be found on the CD-ROM.

19. Copy the entire texture and paste it into your painting. Depending on which layer is active, you will probably need to move the new texture layer down beneath both the face and costume layers. Figure 20.19 shows the painting with the texture pasted in.

20. While a definite improvement over the plain-gray background, there is still room for improvement. The texture as it stands is too light for the figure. There are two solutions to this problem: either we can make the figure lighter or the background darker. As it is easier, we opt to make the background darker. This is very simple to do. Simply change the blend mode to Multiply and use the opacity slider to get a look that you like. There is no right or wrong; just go with your own

**FIGURE 20.17** The initial paint-in of the cape.

personal feeling. Figure 20.20 shows the texture layer changed to Multiply.

21. The painting is now very harmonious in its color scheme. At this point we are in the final cleanup and finish phase. Switching back to the cos-

**FIGURE 20.18**    A texture for the background.

tume layer, the right sleeve is finished and the contours of the costume are cleaned up using a combination of the brush tool we have been using and the Eraser tool. Figure 20.21 shows our progress to this point.

22. Because we have spent most of this tutorial on painting fabric, a few things on the face layer now need to be brought to a finish. We will not spend time on how to make these finishes as this material has been covered in earlier chapters. Switch back to the face layer and finish the hair of the girl as in Figure 20.22. Continue to finish the work on the costume. It should be for the most part complete at this stage.

23. Create a new layer and finish painting the sword as in Figure 20.23. Do any final touchup on the costume and face layers that needs to be done.

**FIGURE 20.19**   A texture pasted into the background.

24. On the texture layer, paint in a subtle light area just to the left of the face to help focus the viewer's attention on the center of interest (Figure 20.24).

25. One last step to add that little something extra to the final image: create a new alpha channel and fill it with a radial gradient as seen in
Figure 20.25. Back in the Layers tab, merge all the visible layers. Now
you have only one layer containing your face, costume, and back-

**FIGURE 20.20**    A texture's blend mode changed to Multiply.

ground. Load a selection from the alpha you created using the gradient. Copy and paste the image back into itself. Change the blend mode of the new layer to Multiply and adjust the opacity to suit you.

**FIGURE 20.21**     The result of finish work to the right sleeve and cleaning up the contours of the costume.

**FIGURE 20.22**    Finishing the hair.

**FIGURE 20.23**    Finishing the sword.

**FIGURE 20.24** Painting a light area in the background just to the left of the face.

**FIGURE 20.25** The alpha channel created and filled with a radial gradient.

The results are seen in Figure 20.26. What you have done is create a very subtle transition of the light that gradually gets darker as you move away from the face and upper body of the figure. This helps accentuate the play of light across the form and leads the eye just where you want. Your image is now finished. ✄

**FIGURE 20.26**    The finished image.

## CONCLUSION

That's about all there is to painting fabric in a very simple way. The most important things to remember when painting this type of subject matter are:

- Simplify and use only three values to do the majority of the painting.
- Draw and paint the fabric with straight lines because as you do additional work, the lines will soften.
- Paint the major folds first, do the smaller folds second, and (if you cannot stand it any longer) add some of the small wrinkles. Remember that the major folds will make the image understandable.
- Vary your values slightly as you paint across the figure.

Almost all costumes may be painted as a variation of this basic technique. Shiny objects will have greater value differences among the three values used. Furry objects will have very soft lines and transitions between shapes. If you analyze your subject carefully and use these simple steps, no costume will be too difficult to paint. In the next chapter, we will be using Photoshop's painting capabilities to paint a man with a sword.

# PAINTING A MAN WITH A SWORD

In this chapter, we will be painting a picture that illustrates the "less is more" concept. Basically, we want to create an image that looks like we spent a lot more time on it than we actually did.

## WHAT YOU NEED TO KNOW ABOUT PHOTOSHOP FOR THIS CHAPTER

The following tutorial assumes that you know some fundamentals of working in Photoshop CS, such as:

- Where individual palettes are located
- How to adjust a brush's opacity
- How to create layers and change their blend mode
- How to resize your brush and sample color from within the image (preferably using the hot keys)
- How to create and use patterns
- How to create brushes

You can arrange the Photoshop workspace to suit your own liking, so this chapter does not discuss where to locate specific items.

**TUTORIAL**

## PAINTING THE IMAGE

The original sketch we will be working from is shown in Figure 21.1.

When you're ready to start painting the man with the sword, follow these steps:

1. Scan the original sketch at 300 dpi so that a good image can be printed directly from the image if you want. The scan was large, almost 3000 pixels in the largest dimension. For the majority of your digital painting, this will be just too cumbersome to start with, so let's resize it to 1500 pixels in the largest dimension. This size is much easier to handle in the initial painting stages. This sketch is located on the CD-ROM if you want to follow along using it or use a sketch of your own.

ON THE CD

*Remember that every image that displayed in these demonstrations represents a saved version of the image. You cannot save enough, so don't hesitate to save constantly. You will be happy in the end that you have gotten into this habit.*

2. Open the image in Photoshop and copy and paste the entire image back into itself. Hide the pasted layer; it will only be used if you need to reestablish your original drawing. As shown in Figure 21.2, render a lighting effect using a slightly blue light. This starts to give the painting the moody feel we want to achieve. Save the image.

**FIGURE 21.1**   The basic sketched drawing.

3. In this image, we want to create something that is dark and creepy, and our goal is to let the viewer's eye fill in many of the details. We need to make the whole thing even darker before we begin painting in earnest. So, we create a new layer, change the blend mode to Multiply, and begin painting in broadly with a dark color using the Airbrush Pen Opacity Flow brush in larger sizes, as shown in Figure 21.3. By using Multiply as the layer's blend mode, we accomplish two

**FIGURE 21.2**    The original sketch with the rendered lighting effect.

**FIGURE 21.3**    Painting on the Multiply layer to darken the image.

things: the image gets darker quickly and we can see the underlying drawing. If we wanted to go darker even quicker, we could change the mode of the brush itself to Multiply. Experiment with these different settings and others to get a look that you like. Save the image.

4. Continue painting all the way down the figure. Notice in Figure 21.4 that we are not worried about staying in the lines of the original drawing. In fact, we are obliterating some of the sketch's original details. This is not important at this stage of the painting. The most important thing is to develop the areas that will be light and those that will be dark. Save the image again.

5. The image is still not dark enough for what we are hoping to accomplish. Merge all the layers except the hidden sketch layer onto the

background, copy the entire image, and paste it back into itself. Then, change the composite method of the layer to Multiply and apply a slight motion blur to make everything look even more mysterious and ambiguous, as shown in Figure 21.5. Save the image.

6. Apply another lighting effect to the base image, as shown in Figure 21.6. We finally get the image dark enough. Save the image.

7. Well, maybe it is actually too dark at this point. Let's somewhat decrease the opacity of the Multiply layer to get it just slightly lighter. Flatten the image down into one layer, and save the image.

**FIGURE 21.4**    Painting down the figure with little concern for the original sketch's details.

**FIGURE 21.5**    The image is two layers at this point, with the top layer having a motion blur applied and the composite method set to Multiply.

8. Just to minimize mistakes, create a new layer and start painting the face using Airbrush Pen Opacity Flow brush in smaller sizes and with greater opacity. We want the face to contrast greatly in both value and color with the rest of the painting. The predominant color theme for the image is in the gold and brown range, so we will make the face very pale and in the blue/purple color range, as shown in Figure 21.7. Save the image

9. Using the same brush, begin to also work into the background areas to help reestablish some of the figure's contours against the background, as shown in Figure 21.8. We are trying very hard to keep our values in their proper place and not visually break apart the flow of the image.

**FIGURE 21.6** Applying another lighting effect to the base layer.

**FIGURE 21.7** Painting the face in blue and purple tones using the Airbrush Pen Opacity Flow brush.

10. Start painting back into the body of the figure using the same Photoshop brush but checking both scatter and texture in the brush options. Increase the Scatter setting and make the brush interact with a texture using the Hard Mix mode. Everything is looking so dark and messy in Figure 21.9 that we begin to wonder if we have ruined the image before we really have started. Flatten the layers and save the image.

ON THE CD

11. Using custom brushes that were created just for this project (and which you can find on the CD-ROM), start painting into the background and into the figure. We want a rather scratchy and nervous look yet we want to use the texture of the brushes to help give the illusion that we

**FIGURE 21.8**  Redefining the edges of the figure.

**FIGURE 21.9**  The painting with a brush that has both Scatter and Texture checked going over the figure's body.

have painted many small details. When using custom brushes with a lot of texture, you will almost always need to increase the scatter of the brush or the textured strokes will run together. It is often also advisable to paint with these brushes as if they are stamps. To do this, simply touch the stylus to the image and lift it off. Do not touch and drag the stylus around. You can see this beginning work in the chest area and above the figure's left shoulder in Figure 21.10. Save the image.

12. Continue to paint the background with multiple different textured brushes. We are sampling color from within the image and are constantly scaling the brushes to get lots of variation. While trying to maintain the golden feeling of the background, start to subtly introduce some cooler color. You can see this best over the figure's right shoulder in Figure 21.11. Try to keep the edges of the image distinct but somewhat ambiguous, as perhaps a ghost would be.

**FIGURE 21.10** The beginning of the texture work into the image.

**FIGURE 21.11** Continued developments in the background textures.

13. Switch brushes to one that has a small round pattern. Sampling some of the darkest colors in the image, paint darks back out into the background over the relatively light color there, as has been done in Figure 21.12. Now and then, switch to the Airbrush Pen Opacity Flow brush and define in some detail the profile of the figure.

14. Using one of the custom brushes that looks like a rocky wall, using a dark color, and scaling the brush up quite large, begin painting a rocky, brick wall behind the figure, as you can see in Figure 21.13. This is one of the areas where it is much easier to let a texture do the majority of the work. We could have drawn the brick wall behind the figure, but since some preliminary time was taken to create a usable brick-like textured brush, we can paint the entire wall in just a few strokes. Save the image.

**FIGURE 21.12**    Changing to different textured brushes and working some dark color into the background.

**FIGURE 21.13**    Painting a brick wall behind the subject using a custom brush made of a brick-like texture.

15. Using Airbrush Pen Opacity Flow, continue to work into the background, adding some lighter and cooler colors. Notice the scratchy line work above the left shoulder in Figure 21.14. Save the image.

16. The hand of the character is going to be significant to the feel that we want to get in the image. Up to this point, we have pretty much ignored refining individual pieces of the image, but now it is appropriate to strengthen the drawing of the left hand. We do not need to draw every finger; just reinforce the silhouette to make sure the hand is recognizable, as shown in Figure 21.15. This work is done with Airbrush Pen Opacity Flow brush.

**FIGURE 21.14** Continued work into the background with Airbrush Pen Opacity Flow to get some variation in color and value.

**FIGURE 21.15** Strengthening the silhouette of the hand.

17. Continue to add more texture and color into the background using custom brushes, particularly around the hand and head areas, as shown in Figure 21.16.
18. Using the same brushes as in the background, begin to paint into the figure itself. We're going for a loose armor look, and we want the impression to be old and almost relic-like. In Figure 21.17, you will notice the most work has been done in the figure's chest area.
19. Using the same custom brushes as before, lighten and paint more (and different) textures into the background surrounding the head and hand. You can see the results in Figure 21.18. Save the image.

**FIGURE 21.16**    Adding more texture and color into the background.

**FIGURE 21.17**    Using textured brushes to start painting armor into the character.

20. Still using a textured brush, but changing the size and opacity as you work, paint in the background and figure. You want to use a brush that is round and somewhat splotchy in texture as it is perfect for adding small, rock-like grains into the image. Figure 21.19 shows the results.

21. We can't wait any longer, so let's add a small bit of red color to the figure's extended figure, as shown in Figure 21.20. Now, as is so important with much character art, we have added a story to the image. What the specific story is about is not nearly as important as the fact that there is a story. We also begin to do some additional work into the wall behind the character, just under the arm.

22. Using the brick-like textured brush, start to add some dimension to the bricks in the wall on the left side of the figure, as shown in Figure 21.21.

**FIGURE 21.18**    More texture work, especially around the head and hand.

**FIGURE 21.19**    Changing to round and blotchy brush texture and continuing to work into the background and figure.

**FIGURE 21.20**    Adding a story to the image by simply adding a bit of red to the extended finger.

**FIGURE 21.21**    Adding some dimension to the rock wall behind the figure.

23. Continue with the same brush and add more dimensional details into the wall on the right side of the figure, as shown in Figure 21.22. We also add some detail in the figure's right arm using the Airbrush Pen Opacity Flow brush in smaller sizes, trying to maintain a random feel. Now this is not real detail but is simply letting the textures already present suggest some detail in the arm.

24. Continue using the Airbrush Pen Opacity Flow brush and paint in some scribbles in both the figure and background. Paint the lines with a very freeform motion, but pay close attention to their direction. In Figure 21.23, we want the strokes to go perpendicular to the form. Once the dark scribbles have been painted in, go in with a lighter color and highlight the edge of them so that they appear to be three-dimensional.

**FIGURE 21.22** Adding more detail into the background and implied detail into the left arm using the Airbrush Pen Opacity Flow brush.

**FIGURE 21.23** Adding "scribble" detail to the image.

25. Do some additional work on the sword and the background around the sword. For the work on the sword, use the Airbrush Pen Opacity Flow brush; when working in the background, use the custom textured brushes. Add a small highlight on the sword, as shown in Figure 21.24. The key here is to not make the sword too light. If we made it lighter, it would punch a visual hole into the image.

26. Using Airbrush Soft Round brush, paint slight highlights on both the figure and the sword, as shown in Figure 21.25.

**FIGURE 21.24**    Painting on the sword and on the background around the sword.

**FIGURE 21.25**    Painting a glow around some of the forehead and sword.

27. For some finishing touches, we'll add a few details on the character's sword handle using the Airbrush Pen Opacity Flow brush, as shown in Figure 21.26.

**FIGURE 21.26**    The finishing touches are placed on the sword's handle.

## CONCLUSION

Well, there you have it: the complete painting from sketch to finish. The goal was to paint a texturally complex image that would look more time consuming than it was. We wanted something that would engage viewers and let them fill in the majority of the details. We also wanted an image that was dark and gothic looking. In the next chapter, we will incorporate most of the techniques we have covered in the last few chapters. We will be painting a "Heaven and Hell" image.

# PAINTING THE "HEAVEN AND HELL" IMAGE

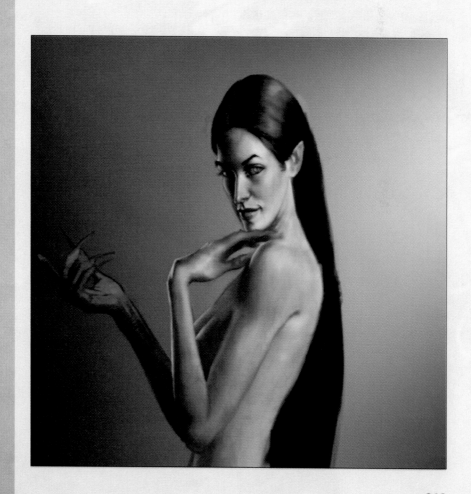

The image "Heaven and Hell," which we will be using in this chapter, was painted for an Internet art contest. The theme was, oddly enough, "Heaven and Hell," and was to be interpreted by the individual artist. It was decided that a new slant on the Christian concept would be used. Some rather traditional symbols were mixed with original ideas, and a model who got into character for both angels was found. After some reference photos were taken, the image was drawn directly on the computer. At the beginning of the process, the final size and resolution of the image were uncertain. The image needed only be viewable at computer screen resolution, but perhaps prints would be made if the finished piece was acceptable.

The demonstration in this chapter follows pretty closely the steps used to create the image. As in all of the demonstrations in this book, we do not take a lot of time to specify specific brush settings or any other of the more mundane aspects of the painting on the computer. These demonstrations are about creating paintings, with all of the flaws and problems that artists encounter, and all the while hoping to have an acceptable end result.

## WHAT YOU NEED TO KNOW ABOUT PHOTOSHOP FOR THIS CHAPTER

The following tutorial assumes that you know some fundamentals of working in Photoshop, such as:

- Where individual palettes are located
- How to adjust a brush's opacity
- How to adjust the grain influence on a brush
- How to create layers and change their blend mode
- How to resize your brush and sample color from within the image (preferably using the hot keys)
- How to create and use patterns
- How to create brushes

You can arrange the Photoshop workspace to suit your own liking, so this chapter does not discuss where to locate specific items.

**TUTORIAL**

## CREATING THE "HEAVEN AND HELL" IMAGE ON THE COMPUTER

When you're ready to start, follow these steps:

1. Create a new document that is approximately 1500 pixels in the largest dimension and fill it with a neutral value gray color. Create a new layer, set the blend mode to Multiply, and sketch your first figure on it. We'll work on hell's angel first, as shown in Figure 22.1.

**FIGURE 22.1**    The sketch of hell's angel.

Perhaps it's easier to approach an evil character than a good one. The image is drawn with the Hard Round 5 brush set to a light gray color. As we draw and refine the image, the color gets progressively darker. We want everything to remain very fluid and subject to change at this early stage; vary the size and opacity of the brush as you need. You will notice in the hair that we have used a larger brush size and darker color. We make the face more angular and sharp, especially the nose. We also make the fingers significantly longer with very long nails. We are trying to have the face's look imply something sinister. Although we have not yet determined the final size of the finished image, we are beginning to get a clear idea about what direction we want the picture to go.

2. We are also beginning to work on the good angel at this point, but on a different layer. We do this mostly to facilitate working on the characters independently later in the painting process. You can see both of the angels in Figure 22.2. This image has two individual layers with an angel on each.

3. Once the general idea for both characters has been developed, hide one of the characters, in this case the good angel. With the bad angel's layer active, hold down the Ctrl button and left-click on the layer to create a selection, and save this selection as an alpha channel. Merge the layer down onto the background, load the selection from the

**FIGURE 22.2**    The two angels back to back.

alpha you just created, and cut and paste the angel back into a new layer. The reason we go through this long process is that the original layer the angels sketch was on had a blend mode set to Multiply and was not suitable for painting on as every stroke would just get darker and darker. Now, the angels sketch will be on a new layer with a blend mode of Normal, which is much more conducive to painting. Begin to paint the bad angel on her individual layer.

4. The background of the image is rather boring and plain at this point. Now is a good time to begin to remedy that problem. Select the background layer and render a lighting effect to this layer. Applying a lighting effect is the easiest way to get some color going in the image. Switch back to the bad angel's layer, and continue painting her. Try to work broadly and with little concern for any outlines that you have drawn. We are not filling in a coloring book; we want to keep the image fluid. Block in the figure and hair, trying to arrive at color and value relationships that will work in the final image. All of this painting is done on the bad angel layer, as seen in Figure 22.3, using the Airbrush Pen Opacity brush at various opacities and sizes.

5. The bad angel is a very bad girl, so for her skin, hair, and eyes use a color scheme that accentuates her rather nasty nature. In this case blacks, grays, and red are perfect for the feeling we are after.

6. Continue your work on the bad angel. Add some cracks into the skin using custom brushes that are available on the CD-ROM. She should have desirable aspects and yet be repulsive at the same time. Cracked skin will be one of her undesirable features, as seen in Figure 22.4.

ON THE CD

**FIGURE 22.3**   Blocking in the bad angel.

**FIGURE 22.4**   Texture is added into the skin.

7. Now we'll reveal the good angel and work on both of the figures concurrently. Depending on how you handled the sketch of the good angel, you may have to go through the same procedure of creating an alpha channel for her layer and then copying and pasting her into a new layer with a Normal blend mode, as described earlier in the chapter. Begin to paint the good angel using the Airbrush Pen Opacity brush. The good angel will be virtually an albino. White is generally characterized as a "good" color, so it is appropriate to our vision of the character to have her very pale; however, we also want the good angel to be creepy in her own right. Since white can also have a ghost-like connotation, she will appear as both good and somewhat creepy at the same time. We'll darken the background around the good angel to help bring out the very pale complexion. Notice in Figure 22.5 that we are not just painting her in grays but that there are many very subtle colors in her skin, including pinks, purples, and blues.

8. We have settled on where the figures will be located in the final image, so we merge their layers together so that both figures are on one layer. We then switch to the background layer and begin developing the colors and feel that we want it to help convey. Notice in Figure 22.6 that we are keeping the background around the bad angel rather warm and that around the good angel rather cool. We have turned off the visibility of the layer where the figures are so that you can see the background work we have done. The background is painted using a variety of brushes and then blended here and there.

9. We have added some rather bright oranges to the left side of the background with the Airbrush Soft Round brush in various sizes. Using the procedure described earlier in Chapter 11, smooth out the

**FIGURE 22.5**    Blocking in the good angel.

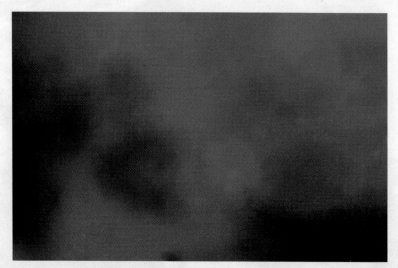

**FIGURE 22.6**    The background layer.

rough areas in the entire background. We are also continuing to work on the two figures. Notice in Figure 22.7 that we have significantly lightened the good angel so that the contrast between the good and bad is extreme.

10. Working on the figure layer, further develop both figures. We work on smoothing out the skin and begin adding some of the details into

**FIGURE 22.7**    The figure layer revealed against the background layer.

the hands and elsewhere. Make sure to get more color into the good angel. In Figure 22.8, you can see this most clearly in the elbows, ears, and other areas of the face.

**FIGURE 22.8**    Notice the strong colors that are added to the figure, which is to appear essentially white.

11. Create a new layer and, as shown in Figure 22.9, add the smoking fire to the dark angel's palm. Paint in the smoke using the Airbrush Soft Round brush in smaller sizes and give it that swirling look by using the Smudge tool. As you start to paint the smoke, keep it brighter and denser close to the hand and gradually make the colors darker as you get farther out. Initially use larger sizes of the smudge tool at higher Strength settings to really move the pixels around. As you get a smoke-like shape, gradually decrease the size and strength of the tool to get finer details.

12. We have added an additional light source, so make sure it shows on the figure. In Figure 22.10, this is most noticeable as bright rim lights on the arms and fingers and even on the face of the dark angel. Use the Airbrush Pen Opacity brush for this work.

13. Continue to refine both figures. Create a new layer and add some clouds into the background behind the white angel. I paint the butterfly on another new layer using mainly airbrushes. The image of a butterfly is used because it symbolically represents both rebirth and resurrection, but personal preferences dictated which specific butterfly was painted. We need to paint only half the butterfly.

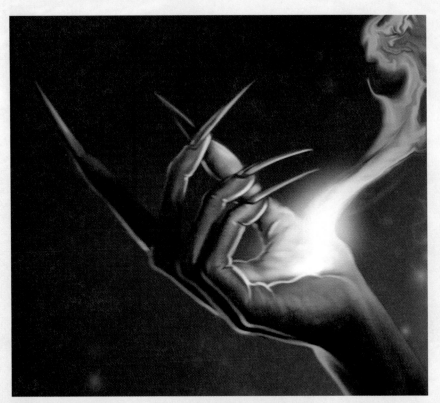

**FIGURE 22.9**    A closeup of the hell angel's smoking palm.

**FIGURE 22.10**    Adding a light source because of the smoking palm.

14. Copy, paste, and flip horizontally half the butterfly we painted so that a complete butterfly is formed. Then hide all layers except the two with the halves of the butterfly, merge both the butterfly layers using the Merge Visible command into one, and then position the butterfly as desired. We have also removed some of the canvas on the right side of the painting.

15. We have decided to add some "hell" by the bad angel, so start painting some of the light that is spilling out of hell onto the edges of both figures. The edge of yellow light that is on the good angel represents how hard it is to keep ourselves separate and aloof from the evils of the world. Figure 22.11 shows the image after we made all these additions.

**FIGURE 22.11** The butterfly, sky layers, and the flames of hell are painted.

16. Now the fun really begins. As you can see in Figure 22.12, we have painted in the flames of hell on the background layer behind the bad angel. We have used a variation of the Airbrush Soft Round brush that has had the Scattering in both axes set very high, along with the size jitter set very high. We also use the Custom brush in a stamping manner to get some of the fiery effects. Most of the flowing flames are painted using the Airbrush Soft Round brush.

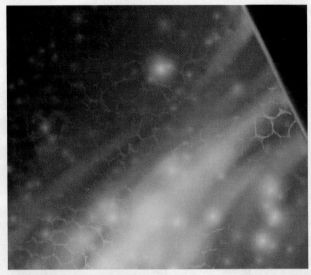

**FIGURE 22.12**   A closeup of the flames.

17. Here is where the use of layers becomes advantageous. We are painting on the background layer and the figures are on the top layer, so we can ignore them completely and concentrate on the flames. We do not have to worry about painting around the figures at all. Figure 22.13 shows the multilayered image where we have painted the flames into the background with complete disregard for the figures on the upper layers.

**FIGURE 22.13**   Painting in the flames.

18. We now need to do a significant amount of work to refine and finish the figures. Figure 22.14 is a closeup of the bad angel's face. Figure 22.15 shows the good angel's face.

**FIGURE 22.14**   A closeup of the bad angel that shows the detail.

19. A lot of work goes into the hair of both characters to make sure that it looks soft and blends correctly into the background. We try to get some brighter colors into both figures. We also work on blending the figures' hair together to visually merge and tie the two figures together. Let's extend the flames farther into the good angel's side of the image, as shown in Figure 22.16.
20. It is only fair if we encroach on heaven's space with fire that we do the same into hell's space with the blue sky. Working in the background layer, paint the sky over into the left side of the image, as shown in Figure 22.17.

**FIGURE 22.15**    A closeup of the good angel's face that shows the use of color and finished detail.

**FIGURE 22.16**    Extending the flames farther into the good angel's background.

**FIGURE 22.17** Painting the sky into the hell angel's side of the image.

21. The painting is almost finished. On a new layer, add the glow and sparkles around the butterfly, as shown in Figure 22.18, using the same variation of the Airbrush Soft Round brush we used on the flames of hell a few steps earlier.

22. We also toy with adding some tattoos and jewelry to the hell figure, as shown in Figure 22.19. Both the jewelry and tattoos are added on a new layer just in case we decide later that we don't like them. At this point, we do not want to have to repaint into the figures at all if we don't have to.

23. It indeed turns out that we've decided we don't like the jewelry or tattoos. Therefore, we delete the layer that they were painted on. The upper-right corner of the picture is rather boring and seems to need something. On a new layer, paint in some darker clouds with the Airbrush Soft Round brush and swirl them using the Smudge tool. On a new layer, we also try the idea of making some light streaking through the clouds. Figure 22.20 shows the results.

24. Again, we change our minds and decide to delete the layer on which the streaks of light in the clouds are painted. After we add an earring on the hell figure, the image is finished, as shown in Figure 22.21. Sometimes knowing when to stop is the hardest thing about painting. Some artists have a tendency to want to continue working until things look overworked. We've stopped at just the right time. 🎨

**FIGURE 22.18**   A closeup of the butterfly with its accompanying glows and sparkles.

**FIGURE 22.19**   Adding jewelry and tattoos to the hell figure.

**FIGURE 22.20** Adding darker clouds, getting rid of the jewelry and tattoos, and making light streak through the clouds.

**FIGURE 22.21** The final painting.

## CONCLUSION

The final painting made use of most of the techniques we discussed in the previous chapters, and we also learned some techniques for what to do when we change our minds. The next chapter shows how to create the image on the front cover of the book. The next chapter will also show how very easy it is to change your mind and make adjustments and corrections when working in the digital world.

# PAINTING THE "WIZARD" IMAGE

The tutorial in this chapter is different from any other in this book. Here, we show the whole process from sketch to final image, including all the backtracks, changes of mind, and errors made while the image was painted.

All of the work in this image was done in Photoshop CS.

## WHAT YOU NEED TO KNOW ABOUT PHOTOSHOP FOR THIS CHAPTER

The following tutorial assumes that you know some fundamentals of working in Photoshop CS, such as:

- Where individual palettes are located
- How to adjust a brush's opacity
- How to create Layer Styles
- How to create layers and change their composite method
- How to resize your brush and sample color from within the image (preferably using the hot keys)
- How to create patterns
- How to create brushes

You can arrange the Photoshop workspace to suit your own liking, so this chapter does not discuss where to locate specific items.

**TUTORIAL**    ## PAINTING THE "WIZARD" IMAGE

When you're ready to start, follow these steps:

ON THE CD

1. Scan the sketch (shown in Figure 23.1) at 300 dpi. Doing so will give you a large enough image for decent prints. The original sketch is available on the CD-ROM if you care to use it instead of a sketch of your own.

2. While in Photoshop, use the Image/Adjustments/Levels command to take away most of the gray in the image. Copy the entire image, cut it, and paste it back as a new layer. Then, change the blend mode of the layer to Multiply so that all of the white becomes clear. You now have an image that has two layers each with a copy of the Wizard sketch on it (Figure 23.2). Hide the top layer. This layer with the sketch will only be used if you need to reestablish your drawing.

3. Create a new layer and name it background. Using the Gradient tool, fill the layer with a Radial Gradient to get rid of all of the bright white, as shown in Figure 23.3. Whether you're painting digitally or traditionally, painting on a white surface only makes your job harder and is simply not a smart thing to do. We will be painting the Wizard

**FIGURE 23.1**    The original sketch.

in blue-purple robes, so we chose the color of the gradient applied to contrast nicely with the cooler colors we will be using. Save the image with the number "02" in the name. We eventually will have a series of images with names containing the number of their development. Right now the layer with the gradient obscures the sketch on

**FIGURE 23.2**   The original sketch after adjusting the levels to get rid of the grays.

the background layer. Change the blend mode of this layer to Multiply. You will notice that the colors in the background do not change. This is because you are multiplying them over white but you are now able to see the sketch on the background layer.

4. Create a new layer and move it so that it is between the top layer (containing the drawing) and the background layer. Using one of Photoshop's brushes, begin to paint in the beard, as shown in Figure 23.4. A good brush to use for this work is the Airbrush Pen Opacity Flow brush at its default settings. Increase either the size, opacity, or both to suit your particular needs. We will be gradually covering the sketch on the background layer with color, but do not be concerned. If you feel we may be losing the drawing, simply turn on the visibility of the top sketch layer. As in traditional painting, we will try to get

**FIGURE 23.3**    Using the Gradient tool with a radial gradient on the layer to get rid of the entire white surface.

some of the lightest lights and darkest darks established quickly so that we know the value range of our painting. Save the image using "03" in the name.

5. Most all of the painting of the Wizard will be on this layer that we have started painting the beard on. We are now going to start painting on the Wizard's face in earnest. Begin painting some detail into the face as you try to refine the features. Notice in Figure 23.5 that we are also beginning to put some of the face color into the hands. It is always a good idea to work across the image when developing the initial painting to help keep the color harmonious. Save the image with "04" in the name.

**FIGURE 23.4** Beginning to paint in the Wizard's beard to establish some lights.

**FIGURE 23.5** Beginning to paint the face a little more clearly.

*You get the idea here that saving is very important. You can assume from this point on that we have saved every image displayed in this demonstration to its individual file; the save instruction will not be repeated.*

6. Using the same brush and making sure that the Face layer is the active layer, continue to refine the features and hands as shown in Figure 23.6. The goal is to take the face, beard, and hands to about 60 percent complete. We do not want to spend more effort to finish them at this point as it makes implementing corrections and changes much harder mentally.

7. Create a new layer, name it robe or some other descriptive name, and begin to work on the Wizard's costume, as shown in Figure 23.7. This layer should be located under the face-beard layer so you will not need to worry about painting around the features we have already

**FIGURE 23.6**    Continuing to work on the face, beard, and hands.

**FIGURE 23.7** A new layer with the beginnings of the costume painted around the face.

painted. In this case, we pick a middle value bluish color that will contrast nicely with the background colors.

8. Continue to paint into the costume, working from the darker values to the lighter ones, as shown in Figure 23.8. We want to make sure that we are using lots of different hues of blue varying to almost violet so that we keep a vibrant and interesting color scheme.

9. Continue to paint the remainder of the robe. As we get farther away from the head, slightly gray the blues. This is for the purpose of keeping the most intense color close to the center of interest, as in Figure 23.9. We do not want to take the painting of the robe to the same degree of finish as the face at this point as there is a much greater chance we will be making additional changes to the painting.

**FIGURE 23.8**    Continue to paint the robe using numerous different hues of blue.

10. You can create a new layer for the next step or work on the robe layer. Begin to paint in some of the decoration on the Wizard's costume, such as the sash around the hat and the belt. The colors are chosen because they are complementary to the blues and purples. Also begin to paint the Wizard's staff, which is in reality a paintbrush. Figure 23.10 shows the results.

11. The Wizard figure is very centrally located at this point. We are going to want to put some background in this image so we will need to move the figure of the Wizard or change the size of the image. In this case, we want to maintain the square format of the painting, so let's move the figure to the right on the picture plane. Using the Move tool, move both the robe layer and the face layer to the right, as

**FIGURE 23.9**   Painting the rest of the robe.

**FIGURE 23.10**   Painting the sash, belt, and staff.

shown in Figure 23.11. For our purposes, it is all right that the bottom of the Wizard's robe goes off the right side of the painting. Make sure that you get your layers aligned as you move them around. We now have a lot more room to put in some background elements to enliven the image.

**FIGURE 23.11**   Moving the face and robe layers to the right of the image.

12. Create a new layer just above the background layer and begin to paint in a table, as shown in Figure 23.12. Do not worry about anything at this point but the basic shape and values.
13. Continue to refine the shape of the table and integrate it more with the figure, as shown in Figure 23.13. Use some of blending techniques described in Chapter 11 to help smooth out our strokes but, once again, do not worry about painting in lots of details at this time.

**FIGURE 23.12** Blocking in an artist table on a new layer.

**FIGURE 23.13** More work on the table.

14. Add some lighter colors right on the edges of the tables to start to give dimension and a feeling of where the light catches in the nicks and dents, as you can see in Figure 23.14. It is important to add this touch of realism to any fantasy painting.

**FIGURE 23.14**    Nicks and dents on the edges of the table.

15. Create a new layer above the table layer. We will paint the paint-mixing pots and the artist's canvas on this layer. Sampling colors from within the image, paint a rough canvas and rough pots and pails, as shown in Figure 23.15. Save the image with the next number in the sequence.

16. Continue to work on the kettle on the floor, the cup, canvas, and plate on the table. It is particularly important to notice the left side of the cup as we have taken blue from within the robe and painted the reflected light using these colors. The more we can use colors from differing areas in the painting in other areas, the greater our color harmony will be. As you can see in Figure 23.16, we also begin to add some designs for visual interest to the kettle and have also continued to refine the table on its layer.

**FIGURE 23.15**    Painting on the canvas and pots on a new layer.

**FIGURE 23.16**    Adding reflected light in the cup and
additional detail in the kettle and table.

17. We make the first editorial change. The paint on the paintbrush looks
a little too much like blood, so we change it to green, as you can see
in Figure 23.17.

**FIGURE 23.17**    Changing the bloody color of the paint on the brush to green.

18. Switching back to the robe layer, continue to refine the costume with more intense color using the Airbrush Pen Opacity Flow brush and blending the colors as they are painted. Paint in the beginnings of the sandals that the Wizard is wearing. We then switch to the face layer and make a change to the character's right hand, making it less a fist by extending the middle finger some. Because we have the figure on a separate layer, we do not have to worry about disturbing the underlying painting. Layers make corrections and changes so very easy. By using the blending technique, we make sure that there are both hard and soft edges throughout the painting. The results are shown in Figure 23.18.

19. Staying on the face layer, we bring the painting of the face and hands to about 80 percent finished. We can do this at this point because we now know for the most part what the completed image is going to look like. Figure 23.19 gives you a closer look at how much more work we have put into these areas.

**FIGURE 23.18**    More work on the costume and changing the gesture of the hand.

**FIGURE 23.19**    A significant amount of work has been done in the hand and face layer.

**FIGURE 23.20**   The whole image with lots of work done in the face and hands.

20. Figure 23.20 shows the whole image at this point in the painting process.
21. We begin to add some of the smaller details in the costume, as shown in Figure 23.21. All of this work is done on a new layer just to make our lives easier should we decide to make changes later in the painting process. We switch back to the robe layer and make a significant change to the Wizard's costume.
22. Because we are making this change on an independent layer, we need not worry about affecting either the face layer or any of the background. If you want to be sure that you will stay in the boundaries of the painted areas, check the small checkered box at the top of the Layers palette as in Figure 23.22. This box is called Lock Trans-

**FIGURE 23.22**
The Lock
Transparent
Pixels box.

**FIGURE 23.21**    Adding decorations to the costume and making a
major change in the costume itself.

parent Pixels and does just what it is labeled. This prevents you from
painting any pixels that are currently transparent.

23. While continuing to paint on the robe layer, we work a significant
amount on the bottom of the robe and the sandals the Wizard is
wearing, as shown in Figure 23.23. We are not really relying on the
original sketch at this point anymore. You can continue to leave the
top sketch layer hidden or delete it at this time. All of our painting
has pretty much covered any of the original image on the background. We will go ahead and merge down the gradient-filled layer
onto the background. Be sure to save the image again.

24. As shown in Figure 23.24, lots of little work is now being done on the
various layers of the image. The beard is rather dark, so we start to add
lighter whites to it up by the face. Up to this point, most of the painting
in the beard has been fairly blocky without trying to imitate the flow of
the hair, so we also start to use strokes that are a bit more like wisps of
hair as we paint into the beard. On the layer where we have been
painting the decorations on the robe, we add additional decorations
hanging from the belt. The overall feel of the painting is not too bright,
so we will also add some intense colors representing paint on the sides

**FIGURE 23.23**    More painting in the robe and sandals.

**FIGURE 23.24**    More work on the beard, decorations on the robe, and paint on the kettle and bowl.

of the kettle and in the bowl on the table. Use short strokes around the jewelry and longer strokes as you get farther from the face.

25. Reestablish some of the folds in the fabric. Add the little face amulet that is hanging from the belt. Don't paint it in completely at this point; just indicate it. Use the blending technique to smooth out the roughness of the canvas leaning against the wall sitting on the table. Go into the background layer and add a large crack going across the image. Notice that the placement of the crack is not random, and its ends lead the viewer to our center of interest, the Wizard's head. Begin to clean up some of the edges of the objects on their individual layers. This can be done using a combination of brushes and the Eraser tool. All of this additional work can be seen in Figure 23.25.

**FIGURE 23.25** Work on the background layer, adding a large crack.

26. Using shorter and choppier strokes, paint some textures into the background to give it some interest. As you can see in Figure 23.26,

**FIGURE 23.26**    Adding a hand-drawn, slightly carved-looking texture to the background.

we try to give the wall a sense of depth and a slightly carved feeling. A bit of work is also done on the floor.

27. We have been ignoring the floor and kettle up to this point, so let's start to give more definition to the kettle sitting on the floor and try to anchor our Wizard onto the floor by refining the painting around his feet. We also add the strings that attach to the amulets that are hanging from the belt. Figure 23.27 shows the results.

28. On a new layer, we add the shadows of the amulets onto the robe to help give a more dimensional feel. As you can see in Figure 23.28, adding these shadows brings the amulets out and away from the robe, adding a touch of dimension.

29. Going back to the face layer, we paint the beard and bushy eyebrows to almost a complete finish. Using the same colors, we go to the layer

**FIGURE 23.27**   Painting the kettle and around the feet of the Wizard.

**FIGURE 23.28**   Shadows are added to the amulets hanging from the Wizard's belt.

with the staff and paint some of the cords around the top of the brush, as shown in Figure 23.29. The last little bit of finish work on these areas will be done in the very final stage of the painting.

**FIGURE 23.29**    The beard is almost finished.

30. Overall, we feel the painting is starting to look pretty good at this point. All of the major color and compositional decisions have been made and settled. We would like to center the attention slightly more on the head of the Wizard and give a little more richness and contrast to the overall image. To do this we will use a technique that we have used before. Create a new alpha channel and fill it with a radial gradient, as in Figure 23.30. The black area should be right over the Wizard's face.

31. Load this alpha channel as a selection, and for each layer of your image, copy and paste a new layer. You will end up with layers that fade from the image at the edges to nothing where the black of the

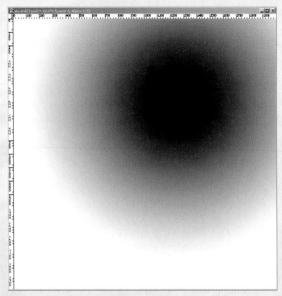

**FIGURE 23.30**   The new alpha channel.

original alpha channel was located in the middle. Set the blend mode for each of the layers to Multiply and adjust the opacity to your liking. This loosely mimics how light works in nature in that it gradually becomes darker as it moves away from the light source. While the Wizard's face is not the actual light source, we can use this phenomenon to lead the eye where we want it to rest. What you will have as a result is an image that fades from a little darker and richer at the edges to what is the original image right over the Wizard's face, giving a visual focal point. Figure 23.31 shows the resulting image. Hide all of the layers and methodically unhide each layer and its corresponding Multiply layer, and using the Merge Visible command, merge each pair of layers. At this time we merge the costume, head, and hands, and any other layers associated with the figure. We do this because we want to start the final finish work on the figure, and it is easier than switching back and forth between different layers.

32. Some major work is under way at this stage. We are trying to finish the robe starting with the hat and working down. Slightly lighter hues and values of blue are painted into the hat and top part of the robe. Careful attention is given to the edges of the robe. A canvas pattern was applied to the canvas on the table using the Filter/Texture/Texturizer filter. The results were too noticeable so we use the Fade command under the Edit menu. That was still not very successful, so we begin to paint over the canvas again. One of the beauties of working digitally is the ability to ex-

**FIGURE 23.31**   The resulting image with each layer selected using the alpha channel and pasted back into the image with a blend mode of Multiply.

periment without the worry of ruining your whole image. This is a good case with that face. Though the texture on the canvas really didn't work, it is easy to change our mind because the rest of the image is left untouched. Figure 23.32 shows the image with these modifications.

33. We make another major change at this stage of the painting. The Wizard's hand on the staff just does not look right so we will move it. One problem: we merged both the costume and head and hands layer. If we had decided to move the hand a few steps earlier it would have been easier as each was on its own layer. Fortunately, the figure is still separate from the background layer so moving the hand will not involve too much work. Make sure that the layer with the figure on it is the active layer. Select the hand using the lasso tool. Either cut or copy the hand and paste it back into the image. Paint the costume up to the pasted

**FIGURE 23.32** More finish on the robe and the canvas mistake.

hand on the original character's layer. Save the image so that you will have a backup image just in case something goes wrong as you merge and paint the repositioned hand and figure layers. When you are happy with the results, merge the two layers as shown in Figure 23.33. Continue working to finish the robe. At this point, it is almost finished down to the waist.

34. Continue to finish the robe and sandals, as shown in Figure 23.34.

35. Finishing is the hardest thing with any painting. At the start the possibilities for greatness are endless. As you paint, decisions are made and sometimes the painting starts to not look as good as you had hoped that it initially would. This is invariably about the spot where we start thinking that the image is never going to look good, and our discouragement runs high. All you can do when you reach this point is continue to carry on and paint. To stop and start something new is counterproduc-

**FIGURE 23.33**    The repositioned hand.

**FIGURE 23.34**    Additional work on the robe and sandals.

tive to actually learning something. You might be surprised but you do learn quite a lot during these hard spots. This does not mean that the image will be beautiful and will become your masterpiece but only that you are learning something valuable for this project and future ones. Our painting looks all right but does not have that sparkle we had hoped it would. What to do? Sometimes when we get to this point it is good to reward ourselves and add some eye candy to our painting. Create a new layer and add the stars to the Wizard's hat and gold trim to his collar (Figure 23.35). Sometimes small touches such as these will revive our vision and encourage us to continue and finish the piece.

**FIGURE 23.35**    Stars and trim added to the costume.

36. Continuing with the idea of adding some eye candy, we add some rings to the Wizard's left hand, as shown in Figure 23.36.
37. Ugh, it has been some time since we have worked on the painting and upon opening the image the Wizard's right hand looks enor-

**FIGURE 23.36**    Painting some rings on the Wizard's fingers.

mous. Not only that, but it is almost centered within the image. While we want the hand to be larger than normal, this is just too large as it is currently painted. Fortunately we do not need to repaint the hand to get it the right size. Once again, painting digitally has saved us a significant amount of work. So, select the hand on the figure's layer, cut and paste the hand back into the image, and scale it to suit your preference. In this case we feel that about 85 percent of the original size is good. Merge the two layers and paint in any of the robe that needs to be repainted to fit the new sized image. Figure 23.37 shows the result of our cut-and-pasting operation.

38. Create a new layer and add a very subtle pattern over the entire background, as shown in Figure 23.38. We don't need to be extremely careful about where we paint the texture because the layer we are painting on is under all but the background layer.

**FIGURE 23.37**    The hand is resized to a more pleasant proportion.

**FIGURE 23.38**    A very subtle texture added to the new layer on top of the background layer.

39. Using the Chalk 44 Pixels brush and on a new layer, paint some modern art on the canvas behind the Wizard. We could paint any type of image we wanted, but there is something very fun about the contrast between a painting so modern against such a medieval character. Figure 23.39 shows the results.

**FIGURE 23.39**    A little modern art added to the canvas in the background.

40. Additional gold trim is added to the robe. This is done on a new layer just in case we do not like the look, but when we are satisfied, immediately merge the two layers into one. The new gold trim can be seen in Figure 23.40.
41. The metallic bowl on the table that was painted over in earlier steps is repainted on a new layer using the Airbrush Opacity Flow brush. Figure 23.41 shows the result.
42. Using the same brush but in smaller sizes, paint the wet purple paint into the bowl with some drips running down the side of the bowl and

**FIGURE 23.40** Gold trim added to the sleeves of the robe.

**FIGURE 23.41** The metallic bowl is repainted on the table.

dripping off the edge of the table, as in Figure 23.42. If we are feeling brave, we can paint these details onto the previous layer, or if we are not as brave, do this on another new layer.

**FIGURE 23.42**    Purple paint is painted into the interior of the bowl.

43. The kettle and cup are finished, as shown in Figure 23.43.
44. The green drips on the kettle, the pinky ring on the Wizard, and his fingernails are now added and finished. We are at a point in our painting where changes are very small and mostly consist of adding the tiny details and cleaning up previous work, as shown in Figure 23.44. For the most part, the work is fairly simple and does not take a lot of explanation except for indicating where the painting is taking place. The remaining steps will be simple descriptions of what is painted, and where.

**FIGURE 23.43**    The kettle and cup are finished.

**FIGURE 23.44**    Green drips, the pinky ring, and the fingernails are painted.

45. A few final touches on the kettle are added in the light side right by the green drips, and the head amulet is finished (Figure 23.45).

**FIGURE 23.45**    Some final touches in the kettle and the finishing work in the amulet.

46. A new layer is added and a lighter texture is painted over the floor area. The Eraser tool is then used to remove any of the painted texture that covers any of the figure or props that sit on the floor. The orange tassels of the belt are painted in with more care. Figure 23.46 shows the resulting image.

47. A rainbow to symbolize the magical aspects of art is added coming from the Wizard's fingers. Creating the rainbow is much easier than it looks. Simply use the gradient tool with a rainbow gradient selected in a radial gradient application. It is important to have transparency at both ends of the gradient so that the rainbow maintains its shape. The gradient used to make this rainbow is located in the folder for this chapter on the CD-ROM. It is easier to draw the gradient in

**FIGURE 23.46** Texture added to the floor and the orange tassels of the belt are painted.

the middle of the new layer and then move the layer so that it is positioned correctly. Using the rectangular selection tool, select the bottom half of the rainbow and delete. You are now left with a very intense rainbow starting at the Wizard's fingers and leading off the canvas, as in Figure 23.47.

48. The rainbow is way too intense. Let's make it more in harmony with the image. To do this we apply a Gaussian Blur under the Filter menu. Play with the slider settings to get the look you are after. This particular rainbow has a blur setting of 18 pixels. Once we have blurred the rainbow, decrease its opacity in the Layers palette to about 50 percent. The results are shown in Figure 23.48. Save your image.

49. The image is for the most part complete at this point. We are going to do one last thing and that is add some sparkles off the end of the Wizard's finger. To do this, create a new layer and paint a few sparkles using a customized airbrush. Customize the brush by changing the

**FIGURE 23.47**    A very intense rainbow added to the image.

**FIGURE 23.48**    Blurring and decreasing the opacity of the rainbow.

ON THE CD

scatter, size variation, and hue jitter until you get a look that you like. If you don't want to customize your own brush, use a brush set called Sparkles in the folder for this chapter on the CD-ROM. Paint a number of sparkly dots and change the blend mode of the layer to either Vivid Light or Linear Light to increase their intensity. Figure 23.49 shows the image with the sparkles added; this is also the final image. ❧

**FIGURE 23.49** Sparkles added and the final image.

## CONCLUSION

This is one of the more complicated digital paintings that you may attempt. It may not end up being a good painting, but you will have learned a great deal while doing it. The image of the "Wizard" is the last demonstration in the book because it's important to show the complete process of digital painting, including the mistakes and explorations that go into creating an image. We hope that seeing the entire process will spur your own experimentation and help eliminate any fear you may have of trying something new.

# ABOUT THE CD-ROM

**Chapter 11 folder:** Contains the image are used in the example demonstrated in Chapter 11.

**Chapter 12 folder:** Contains three different texture images that are used in the examples demonstrated in Chapter 12.

**Chapter 13 folder:** Contains the texture used in the chapter to demonstrate the use of a texture in making a Photoshop brush.

**Chapter 17 folder:** Contains the original sketch, which is used in the demonstration. The folder also contains two custom brush libraries used in the tutorial.

**Chapter 18 folder:** Contains the original sketch to use when following the tutorial. Also contains two custom brush libraries used in the tutorial and 20 custom swatches palettes to use in your own projects.

**Chapter 19 folder:** Contains the original sketch used as the basis of the painting as well as two brush libraries to use.

**Chapter 20 folder:** Contains the original sketch used in the Chapter 20 tutorial painting.

**Chapter 21 folder:** Contains the original sketch used in the tutorial along with two brush libraries.

**Chapter 22 folder:** Contains the file needed to create a pattern used in the tutorial.

**Chapter 23 folder:** Contains the original sketch used in the painting as well as a custom gradient needed to create the rainbow effect. Also contains the Sparkle brush.

**Brushes folder:** Contains all of the custom brushes and more in their rough state that were used in the painting tutorials of each chapter. These brushes are compatible for both the Mac and PC.

**Textures folder:** Contains 137 different textures for you to experiment with when making your own pattern and brush files.

**Software folder:** Contains the Mac and PC tryout versions of Photoshop CS.

## WHAT IS PHOTOSHOP?

Photoshop is the premiere digital imaging tool available. Additional information can be found at:

*www.adobe.com*
Toll-Free Number
800-833-6687

U.S. and Canadian customers can get recorded information about how to order products, determine the status of an order, or contact a customer service representative.

San Jose Corporate Headquarters
Adobe Systems Inc.
345 Park Avenue
San Jose, California 95110-2704
Tel: 408-536-6000
Fax: 408-537-6000

If you have any trouble installing or using the demonstration please contact Adobe Technical Support at *www.adobe.com/supportmain.htm/*

It is hoped that you will find something of use and pleasure when using the CD-ROM.

## SYSTEM REQUIREMENTS

### Windows

- Intel Pentium III or 4 processor
- Microsoft Windows 2000 with Service Pack 3 or Windows XP
- 192 MB RAM
- 280 MB of available hard-disk space
- Color monitor with 16-bit color or greater video card

- 1,024 x 768 or greater resolution
- CD-ROM drive
- Internet or phone connection required for product activation

## Macintosh

- PowerPC G3, G4, or G5 processor
- Mac OS X v.10.2.4 through v.10.3 with Java Runtime Environment 1.4
- 192 MB RAM
- 320 MB of available hard-disk space
- 1,024 x 768 or greater resolution
- CD-ROM drive

# INDEX